Directed Reading A

Section: Development of the Atomic Theory

THE BEGINNING OF ATOMIC THEORY

_______ **1.** The word *atom* comes from the Greek word *atomos*, which means
   a. "dividable."
   b. "invisible."
   c. "hard particles."
   d. "not able to be divided."

_______ **2.** Which of the following statements is a part of Democritus's theory about atoms?
   a. Atoms are small, soft particles.
   b. Atoms are always standing still.
   c. Atoms are made of a single material.
   d. Atoms are small particles that can be cut in half again and again.

3. We know that Democritus was right to say that all matter was made up of atoms. So why did people ignore Democritus's ideas for such a long time?

____

____

____

4. The smallest unit of an element that maintains the properties of that element

is a(n) _____________________.

DALTON'S ATOMIC THEORY BASED ON EXPERIMENTS

_______ **5.** Which of the following was NOT one of Dalton's theories?
   a. All substances are made of atoms.
   b. Atoms of the same element are exactly alike.
   c. Atoms of different elements are alike.
   d. Atoms join with other atoms to make new substances.

6. Dalton experimented with different substances. What did his results suggest?

____

____

____

THOMSON'S DISCOVERY OF ELECTRONS

7. In Thomson's experiments with a cathode-ray tube, he discovered that a(n)

_______________________ charged plate attracted the beam. He concluded

that the beam was made up of particles that have _______________________

electric charges.

8. The negatively charged subatomic particles that Thomson discovered

are now called _______________________.

9. In Thomson's "plum-pudding" model, electrons are mixed throughout an

_______________________.

RUTHERFORD'S ATOMIC "SHOOTING GALLERY"

_______**10.** Before his experiment, what did Rutherford expect the particles to do?
  a. He expected the particles to pass right through the gold foil.
  b. He expected the particles to deflect to the sides of the gold foil.
  c. He expected the particles to bounce straight back.
  d. He expected the particles to become negatively charged.

11. What were the surprising results of Rutherford's gold-foil experiment?

____

____

____

WHERE ARE THE ELECTRONS?

_______**12.** In 1911, Rutherford revised the atomic theory. Which of the following
  is NOT part of that theory?
  a. Most of the atom's mass is in its nucleus.
  b. The nucleus is a tiny, dense, positively charged region.
  c. Positively charged particles that pass close by the nucleus are
      pushed away by the positive charges in the nucleus.
  d. The nucleus is made up of protons and electrons.

13. The center of an atom is a dense region consisting of protons and neutrons

called the _______________________.

14. What are electron clouds?

____

Directed Reading A

Section: The Atom
HOW SMALL IS AN ATOM?

_______ **1.** Which of the following statements is true?
   a. A penny has about 20,000 atoms.
   b. A penny has more atoms than Earth has people.
   c. Aluminum is made up of large-sized atoms.
   d. Aluminum atoms have a diameter of about 3 cm.

WHAT'S INSIDE AN ATOM?

Match the correct description with the correct term. Write the letter in the space provided.

_______ **2.** particle of the nucleus that has no electrical charge

_______ **3.** particle found in the nucleus that is positively charged

_______ **4.** particle with an unequal number of protons and electrons

_______ **5.** negatively charged particle found outside the nucleus

_______ **6.** contains most of the mass of an atom

_______ **7.** SI unit used for the masses of atomic particles

a. electron

b. atomic mass unit (amu)

c. nucleus

d. proton

e. ion

f. neutron

HOW DO ATOMS OF DIFFERENT ELEMENTS DIFFER?

8. The simplest atom is the _______________________ atom. It has one

_______________________ and one _______________________.

9. Neutrons in the atom's _______________________ keep two or more protons from moving apart.

10. If you build an atom using two protons, two neutrons, and two electrons, you

have built an atom of _______________________.

11. An atom does not have to have equal numbers of _______________________

and _______________________.

Directed Reading A *continued*

12. The number of protons in the nucleus of an atom is the

_________________________________ of that atom.

ISOTOPES

______**13.** Isotopes always have
    a. the same number of protons.
    b. the same number of neutrons.
    c. a different atomic number.
    d. the same mass.

______**14.** Which of the following is NOT true about unstable atoms?
    a. They are radioactive.
    b. They have a nucleus that always remains the same.
    c. They give off energy as they fall apart.
    d. They give off smaller particles as they fall apart.

______**15.** What is the mass number of an isotope that has 5 protons, 6 neutrons, and 5 electrons?
    a. 1   **c.** 10
    b. 11   **d.** 16

______**16.** If carbon has an atomic number of 6, how many neutrons does carbon-12 have?
    a. 12   **c.** 6
    b. 8   **d.** 18

17. Most elements contain a mixture of two or more _________________________.

18. The weighted average of the masses of all the naturally occurring isotopes of

an element is the _________________________.

FORCES IN ATOMS

Match the correct definition with the correct term. Write the letter in the space provided.

______**19.** helps protons stay together in the nucleus   **a.** gravitational force

______**20.** pulls objects toward one another   **b.** electromagnetic force

______**21.** an important force in radioactive atoms   **c.** strong force

______**22.** holds the electrons around the nucleus   **d.** weak force

Directed Reading B

Section: Development of the Atomic Theory
THE BEGINNING OF ATOMIC THEORY

Circle the letter of the best answer for each question.

1. What does the word atom mean?

   a. "dividable"

   b. "invisible"

   c. "hard particles"

   d. "not able to be divided"

2. Why weren't Democritus's ideas accepted?

   a. Bohr did not agree with his theory.

   b. Dalton proved Democritus wrong.

   c. Aristotle did not agree with his theory.

   d. Rutherford proved Democritus wrong.

From Aristotle to Modern Science

3. What is the smallest particle into which an element can be divided?

   a. a nucleus

   b. a proton

   c. an atom

   d. a neutron

DALTON'S ATOMIC THEORY BASED ON EXPERIMENTS

4. Which of the following ideas was part of Dalton's theories?

   a. All substances are made of atoms.

   b. Atoms can be divided.

   c. Atoms can be destroyed.

   d. Most substances are made of atoms.

Not Quite Correct

<u>Circle the letter</u> of the best answer for each question.

5. What happened in the late 1800s?

    a. Dalton created a new theory.

    b. Dalton disproved his own theory.

    c. Dalton's theory was proved.

    d. Dalton's theory changed.

THOMSON'S DISCOVERY OF ELECTRONS

Read the words in the box. Read the sentences. <u>Fill in each blank</u> with the word or phrase that best completes the sentence.

electrons	particles
cathode-ray tube	positively

6. Thomson experimented with a ________________________________.

7. Thomson discovered that a ________________________________

charged plate attracted the beam.

8. Thomson concluded that the beam was made of

________________________________ that have negative electric charges.

9. The negatively charged particles Thompson discovered are called

________________________________.

Like Plums in a Pudding

Circle the letter of the best answer for each question.

10. What did Thomson believe about electrons?

   a. They are mixed throughout an atom.

   b. They are in the center of an atom.

   c. They are positively charged.

   d. They are absent from an atom.

RUTHERFORD'S ATOMIC "SHOOTING GALLERY"
Surprising Results

11. What did Rutherford expect the particles to do?

   a. to pass right through the gold foil

   b. to deflect to the sides of the gold foil

   c. to bounce straight back

   d. to become "blobs" of matter

WHERE ARE THE ELECTRONS?

12. Which of the following statements is NOT true of Rutherford's results?

   a. Some of the particles turned to one side.

   b. some of the particles did not move.

   c. Most of the particles passed through the gold foil.

   d. Some of the particles bounced straight back.

13. What is an atom is made up of?

   a. mostly empty space.

   b. helium.

   c. gold particles.

   d. large particles.

| Directed Reading B *continued*

Far From the Nucleus
Circle the letter of the best answer for each question.

14. What did Rutherford believe was in the center of an atom?

    a. an electron

    b. a nucleus

    c. a particle

    d. a proton

BOHR'S ELECTRON LEVELS

15. What did Bohr study?

    a. the way atoms react to light

    b. the size of atoms

    c. the diameter of the nucleus

    d. the division of atoms

16. How did Bohr's model propose that electrons move around the nucleus?

    a. a variety of ways

    b. haphazardly

    c. between the levels

    d. in certain paths

The Modern Atomic Theory

17. What model represents current atomic theory?

    a. electron-cloud model

    b. plum-pudding model

    c. Rutherford's model

    d. Bohr's model

Directed Reading B

Section: The Atom
HOW SMALL IS AN ATOM?
Circle the letter of the best answer for the question.

1. Which of the following statements is true?

   a. A penny has about 20,000 atoms.

   b. A penny has more atoms than the Earth has people.

   c. Aluminum is made up of large-sized atoms.

   d. Aluminum has a diameter of about 3 cm.

WHAT'S INSIDE AN ATOM?
The Nucleus

Read the description. Then, draw a line from the dot next to each description to the matching word.

2. particle with no electrical charge   ●

     a. electron

3. particle that is positively charged   ●

     b. nucleus

     c. proton

4. particle that is negatively charged   ●

     d. neutron

5. contains most of the mass of an atom   ●

HOW DO ATOMS OF DIFFERENT ELEMENTS DIFFER?

Starting Simply

Read the words in the box. Read the sentences. <u>Fill in each blank</u> with the word or phrase that best completes the sentence.

helium	hydrogen	atomic mass unit
neutrons	atomic number	electron

6. The simplest atom is the _________________________ atom. It

has one proton and one _________________________.

Now for Some Neutrons

7. If you build an atom using two protons, two neutrons, and two electrons, you have built an atom of

_________________________.

Building Bigger Atoms

8. An atom does not have to have equal numbers of protons and

_________________________.

Protons and the Atomic Number

9. The number of protons in the nucleus of an atom is the

_________________________ of that atom.

10. The SI unit used to express the masses of particles in atoms is

called the _________________________.

Directed Reading B *continued*

ISOTOPES

Circle the letter of the best answer for each question.

11. What do isotopes always have?

    a. the same number of protons

    b. the same number of neutrons

    c. a different atomic number

    d. the same mass

12. How are isotopes of the same element different?

    a. They have different numbers of protons.

    b. They have different numbers of neutrons.

    c. They have the same number of electrons.

    d. They have different numbers of ions.

Properties of Isotopes

13. Which phrase best describes radioactive isotopes?

    a. They are stable.

    b. They never change.

    c. They are unstable.

    d. They don't produce energy.

Telling Isotopes Apart

14. What is the mass number of an isotope that has 5 protons, 6 neutrons, and 5 electrons?

    a. 1   **c.** 10

    b. 11   **d.** 16

Naming Isotopes

15. Carbon has an atomic number of 6. How many neutrons does carbon-12 have?

    a. 12   **c.** 6

    b. 8   **d.** 18

Directed Reading B *continued*

Calculating the Mass of an Element

Read the words in the box. Read the sentences. <u>Fill in each blank</u> with the word or phrase that best completes the sentence.

mass number	atomic mass

16. The sum of the protons and neutrons in an atom is the

_________________________________.

17. The weighted average of the masses of all the naturally occurring

isotopes of an element is the _________________________.

FORCES IN ATOMS

strong force	electromagnetic force
weak force	gravitational force

18. Protons stay together in the nucleus because of

_________________________________.

19. Objects are pulled toward one another because of

_________________________________.

20. An important force in radioactive atoms is

_________________________________.

21. The electrons are held around the nucleus because of

_________________________________.

Vocabulary and Section Summary

Development of the Atomic Theory
VOCABULARY

In your own words, write a definition of the following terms in the space provided.

1. atom

2. electron

3. nucleus

4. electron cloud

SECTION SUMMARY

Read the following section summary.

- Democritus thought that matter is composed of atoms.
- Dalton based his theory on observations of how elements combine.
- Thomson discovered electrons in atoms.
- Rutherford discovered that atoms are mostly empty space with a dense, positive nucleus.
- Bohr proposed that electrons are located in levels at certain distances from the nucleus.
- The electron-cloud model represents the current atomic theory.

Skills Worksheet

Vocabulary and Section Summary

The Atom
VOCABULARY

In your own words, write a definition of the following terms in the space provided.

1. proton

____

____

2. atomic mass unit

____

____

3. neutron

____

____

4. atomic number

____

____

5. isotope

____

____

6. mass number

____

____

7. atomic mass

____

____

▌Vocabulary and Section Summary *continued*

SECTION SUMMARY

Read the following section summary.

- Atoms are extremely small. Ordinary-sized objects are made up of very large numbers of atoms.

- Atoms consist of a nucleus, which has protons and usually neutrons, and electrons, located in electron clouds around the nucleus.

- The number of protons in the nucleus of an atom is that atom's atomic number. All atoms of an element have the same atomic number.

- Different isotopes of an element have different numbers of neutrons in their nuclei. Isotopes of an element share most chemical and physical properties.

- The mass number of an atom is the sum of the atom's neutrons and protons.

- Atomic mass is a weighted average of the masses of natural isotopes of an element.

- The forces at work in an atom are gravitational force, electromagnetic force, strong force, and weak force.

Skills Worksheet)

Section Review

Development of the Atomic Theory
USING KEY TERMS

1. In your own words, write a definition for the term *atom*.

____

____

2. Use the following terms in the same sentence: *theory* and *model*.

____

____

The statements below are false. For each statement, replace the underlined term to make a true statement.

3. A(n) <u>nucleus</u> is a particle with a negative electric charge.

____

4. The <u>electron</u> is where most of an atom's mass is located.

____

UNDERSTANDING KEY IDEAS

_______ **5.** Which of the following scientists discovered that atoms contain electrons?
   a. Dalton
   b. Thomson
   c. Rutherford
   d. Bohr

6. What did Dalton do in developing his theory that Democritus did not do?

____

____

7. What discovery demonstrated that atoms are mostly empty space?

____

____

| Section Review *continued*

CRITICAL THINKING

8. Making Comparisons Compare the location of electrons according to Bohr's theory and to the current atomic theory.

____

____

____

____

9. Analyzing Methods How does the design of Rutherford's experiment show what he was trying to find out?

____

____

____

____

INTERPRETING GRAPHICS

10. What about the atomic model shown below was shown to be incorrect?

____

____

____

____

Skills Worksheet)

Section Review

The Atom

USING KEY TERMS

1. Use the following terms in the same sentence: *proton*, *neutron*, and *isotope*.

____

____

Complete each of the following sentences by choosing the correct term from the word bank.

atomic mass unit	atomic number
mass number	atomic mass

2. An atom's _____________________ is equal to the number of protons in its nucleus.

3. An atom's _____________________ is equal to the weighted average of the masses of all the naturally occurring isotopes of that element.

UNDERSTANDING KEY IDEAS

_______ **4.** Which of the following particles has no electric charge?
    a. proton   **c.** electron
    b. neutron   **d.** ion

5. Name and describe the four forces that are at work within the nucleus of an atom.

____

____

____

MATH SKILLS

6. The metal thallium occurs naturally as 30% thallium-203 and 70% thallium-205. Calculate the atomic mass of thallium. Show your work below.

Section Review *continued*

CRITICAL THINKING

7. Analyzing Ideas Why is gravitational force in the nucleus so small?

____

____

____

____

8. Predicting Consequences Could a nucleus of more than one proton but no neutrons exist? Explain.

____

____

____

____

INTERPRETING GRAPHICS

9. Look at the two atomic models below. Do the two atoms represent different elements or different isotopes? Explain.

____

____

____

____

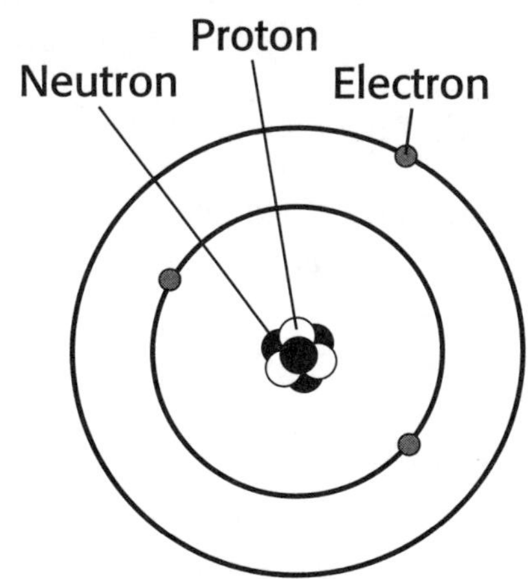

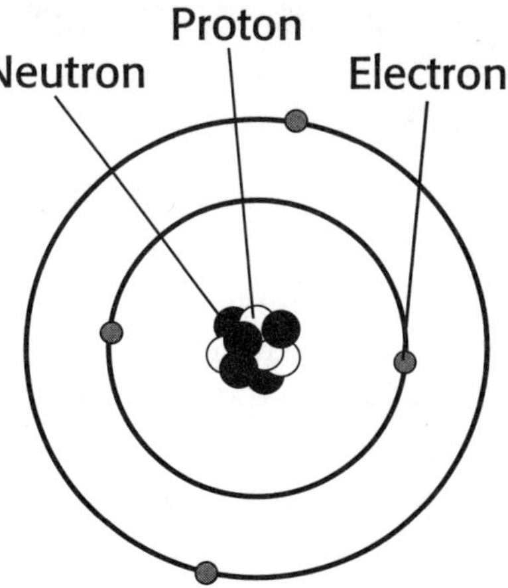

Chapter Review

USING KEY TERMS

The statements below are false. For each statement, replace the underlined term to make a true statement.

1. <u>Electrons</u> have a positive charge.

____

2. All atoms of the same element contain the same number of <u>neutrons</u>.

____

3. <u>Protons</u> have no electrical charge.

____

4. The <u>atomic number</u> of an element is the number of protons and neutrons in the nucleus.

____

5. The <u>mass number</u> is an average of the masses of all naturally occurring isotopes of an element.

____

UNDERSTANDING KEY IDEAS

Multiple Choice

_______ 6. The discovery of which particle proved that the atom is not indivisible?
  a. proton   **c.** electron
  b. neutron   **d.** nucleus

_______ 7. How many protons does an atom with an atomic number of 23 and a mass number of 51 have?
  a. 23   **c.** 51
  b. 28   **d.** 74

_______ 8. In Rutherford's gold-foil experiment, Rutherford concluded that the atom is mostly empty space with a small, massive, positively charged center because
  a. most of the particles passed straight through the foil.
  b. some particles were slightly deflected.
  c. a few particles bounced straight back.
  d. All of the above

Chapter Review *continued*

_______ **9.** Which of the following determines the identity of an element?
  a. atomic number
  b. mass number
  c. atomic mass
  d. overall charge

_______ **10.** Isotopes exist because atoms of the same element can have different numbers of
  a. protons.
  b. neutrons.
  c. electrons.
  d. None of the above

Short Answer

11. What force holds electrons in atoms?

____

____

12. In two or three sentences, describe Thomson's plum-pudding model of the atom.

____

____

____

Math Skills

13. Calculate the atomic mass of gallium, which consists of 60% gallium-69 and 40% gallium-71. Show your work below.

14. Calculate the number of protons, neutrons, and electrons in an atom of zirconium-90 that has no overall charge and an atomic number of 40. Show your work below.

Chapter Review *continued*

CRITICAL THINKING

15. Concept Mapping Use the following terms to create a concept map: *atom, nucleus, protons, neutrons, electrons, isotopes, atomic number,* and *mass number.*

▌Chapter Review *continued*

16. Analyzing Processes Particle accelerators, are devices that speed up charged particles in order to smash them together. Scientists use these devices to make atoms. How can scientists determine whether the atoms formed are a new element or a new isotope of a known element?

____

____

____

____

17. Analyzing Ideas John Dalton made a number of statements about atoms that are now known to be incorrect. Why do you think his atomic theory is still found in science textbooks?

____

____

____

____

18. Analyzing Methods If scientists had tried to repeat Thomson's experiment and found that they could not, would Thomson's conclusion still have been valid? Explain your answer.

____

____

____

____

| Chapter Review *continued*

INTERPRETING GRAPHICS

Use the diagrams below to answer the questions that follow.

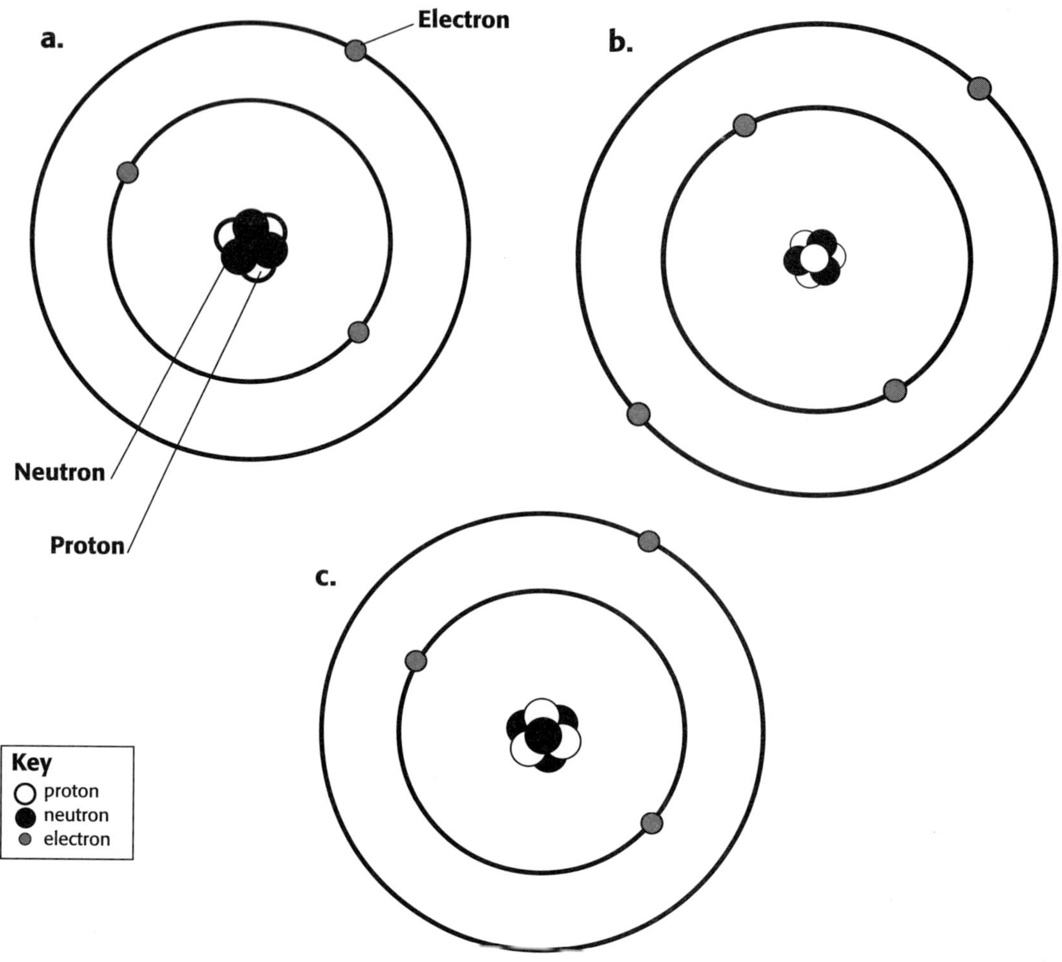

19. Which diagrams represent isotopes of the same element?

____

____

20. What is the atomic number for A?

____

____

21. What is the mass number for B?

____

____

Name _________________________________ Class _______________ Date _____________

Reinforcement

Atomic Timeline

Complete this worksheet after you have finished reading the section "Development of the Atomic Theory."

The table below contains a number of statements connected to major discoveries in the development of atomic theory.

1. In each box, write the name of the scientist(s) associated with the statement. Choose from among the following scientists: Democritus, Rutherford, Thomson, Dalton, Bohr, Schrödinger, and Heisenberg.

2. On a separate sheet of paper, construct a timeline, and label the following: 440 BCE, 1803, 1897, 1909–1911, 1913, and the twentieth century. Cut out the boxes and tape or glue each box at the correct point along the timeline.

A. Most of an atom's mass is in the nucleus.	**B.** There is a small, dense, positively charged nucleus.
C. There are small, negatively charged particles inside an atom.	**D.** Electrons can jump from a path in one level to a path in another level.
E. Atoms of different elements are different.	**F.** He conducted the cathode-ray tube experiment.
G. Atoms are small, hard particles.	**H.** Atoms contain mostly empty space.
I. Atoms are "uncuttable."	**J.** He conducted experiments in combining elements.
K. Electrons travel in certain paths, or energy levels.	**L.** Electron paths cannot be predicted.
M. His theory of atomic structure led to the "plum-pudding" model.	**N.** His model had electrons surrounding the nucleus at a distance.
O. Atoms of the same element are exactly alike.	**P.** Electrons are found in electron clouds, not paths.
Q. All substances are made of atoms.	**R.** Atoms are made of a single material formed into different shapes and sizes.
S. He conducted the gold foil experiment.	**T.** He wanted to know why elements combine in specific proportions.

Critical Thinking

Incredible Shrinking Scientist!

You have received the following E-mail from a friend:

You'll never believe what happened today! My boss, Professor Pat Pending, was accidentally shrunk by her own invention, the "shrinking ray." In order to return her to her normal size, I tried to find her by using a super-high-powered microscope. I found the professor near the nucleus of an oxygen atom. Luckily, she was wearing a specially designed suit that carries an electrical charge. As I watched, I noticed something strange: The professor seemed to be traveling outward, as if she were being pushed away from the nucleus. Her lab notebook mentioned that contact must be made with a carbon-14 isotope to reverse the shrinking process. I'll write you tomorrow with an update.

UNDERSTANDING CONCEPTS

1. What was the charge on the professor's suit when she was moving away from the nucleus? How do you know?

____

____

____

____

2. If the professor had lacked movement toward or away from the nucleus, what would the charge on her suit have been?

____

____

____

____

3. How might other forces inside the atom affect the professor? Explain your answer.

____

____

____

____

| Critical Thinking *continued*

COMPREHENDING IDEAS

4. How could Professor Pending identify a carbon atom at the subatomic level?

____

____

____

5. How can Professor Pending use the concept of mass number to identify a carbon-14 isotope?

____

____

____

6. How many electrons would be needed to make the carbon-14 isotope a negatively charged ion?

____

____

____

MAKING COMPARISONS

7. The Earth and moon have a relationship that could be compared with the nucleus and electron of a simple atom. Describe the similarities and differences between these relationships. Write your answers below. Discuss your answers in groups.

____

____

____

____

Section Quiz

Section: Development of the Atomic Theory

Write the letter of the correct answer in the space provided.

_______ **1.** The smallest particle into which an element can be divided and still be
the same substance is called a(n)
   a. nucleus.
   b. electron.
   c. atom.
   d. neutron.

_______ **2.** What particle did J. J. Thomson discover?
   a. neutron
   b. electron
   c. atom
   d. proton

_______ **3.** How would you describe the nucleus?
   a. dense, positively charged
   b. large, positively charged
   c. tiny, negatively charged
   d. dense, negatively charged

_______ **4.** Where are electrons *likely* to be found?
   a. the nucleus
   b. electron clouds
   c. mixed throughout an atom
   d. paths, or energy levels

_______ **5.** Dalton believed that
   a. atoms of the same element are exactly alike.
   b. most substances are made of atoms.
   c. atoms of different elements are the same.
   d. atoms can be divided.

Section Quiz

Section: The Atom

Match the correct definition with the correct term. Write the letter in the space provided.

_______ **1.** particle of the nucleus with no electrical charge

_______ **2.** negatively charged particle

_______ **3.** keeps a nucleus with two or more protons from flying apart

_______ **4.** subatomic particle that has a positive charge

_______ **5.** pulls objects toward one another

_______ **6.** atom that has the same number of protons as other atoms of the same element do but that has a different number of neutrons

_______ **7.** a charged atom that forms when the numbers of electrons and protons are not equal

_______ **8.** represents the sum of protons in the nucleus of an atom

_______ **9.** enables a neutron to change into a proton and an electron in certain unstable atoms

_______ **10.** the sum of the protons and neutrons in an atom

a. atomic number

b. proton

c. strong force

d. neutron

e. isotope

f. mass number

g. weak force

h. ion

i. electron

j. gravitational force

Chapter Test A

Introduction to Atoms
MULTIPLE CHOICE
Write the letter of the correct answer in the space provided.

_______ **1.** What did Democritus, Dalton, Thomson, Rutherford, and Bohr all have in common?
  a. They each identified new elements.
  b. They each identified new isotopes of atoms.
  c. They each contributed to the development of the atomic theory.
  d. They each conducted experiments in which particles collided.

_______ **2.** In Thomson's "plum-pudding" model of the atom, the plums represent
  a. atoms.   **c.** neutrons.
  b. protons.   **d.** electrons.

_______ **3.** An atom of gold with 79 protons, 79 electrons, and 118 neutrons would have a mass number of
  a. 39.   **c.** 197.
  b. 158.   **d.** 276.

_______ **4.** Which of the following has the least mass?
  a. nucleus   **c.** neutron
  b. proton   **d.** electron

_______ **5.** If an isotope of uranium, uranium-235, has 92 protons, how many protons does uranium-238 have?
  a. 92   **c.** 143
  b. 95   **d.** 146

_______ **6.** How did Democritus describe atoms?
  a. large, soft particles
  b. dividable particles
  c. small, hard particles
  d. a single material with one shape and size

_______ **7.** What is the smallest particle into which an element can be divided and still be the same substance?
  a. electron   **c.** proton
  b. neutron   **d.** atom

Chapter Test A *continued*

MATCHING

Match the correct description with the correct term. Write the letter in the space provided.

_______ **8.** particle than cannot be cut

_______ **9.** negatively charged particle discovered by Thomson

_______ **10.** central region of the atom

_______ **11.** region where electrons are likely to be found

_______ **12.** particle in the center of an atom that has no charge

_______ **13.** subatomic particle that has a positive charge

_______ **14.** a unit of mass that describes the mass of an atom or molecule

_______ **15.** the number of protons in the nucleus of an atom

_______ **16.** atom that has the same number of protons but different numbers of neutrons

_______ **17.** the sum of protons and neutrons in an atom

a. atomic number

b. nucleus

c. electron cloud

d. mass number

e. isotope

f. neutron

g. atom

h. electron

i. atomic mass unit (amu)

j. proton

| Chapter Test A *continued*

MATCHING

Use the diagram below to answer questions 18 through 21. Write the letter of the correct answer in the space provided.

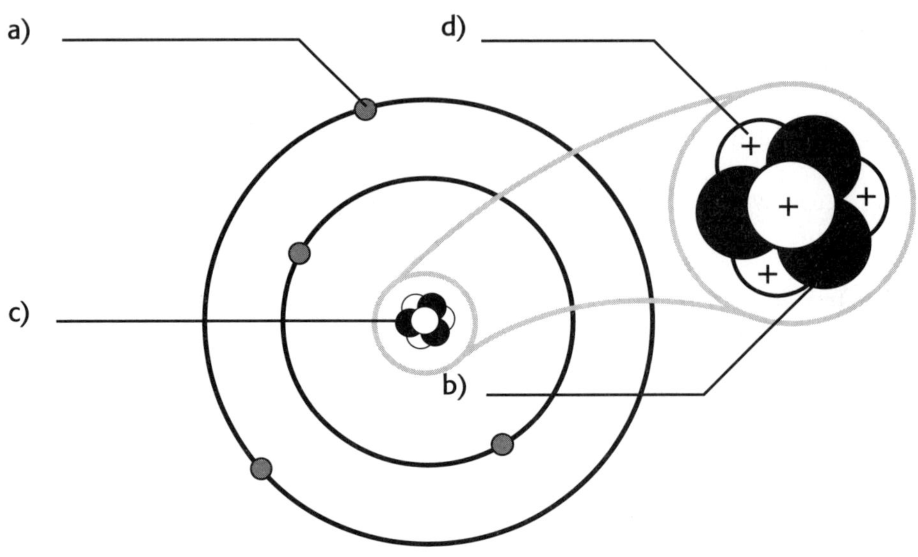

_______**18.** Which letter refers to the negatively charged particles?

_______**19.** Which letter refers to the positively charged particles?

_______**20.** Which letter refers to the particles with no charge?

_______**21.** Which letter refers to the dense center of the atom?

MULTIPLE CHOICE

Use the figure below to answer the questions 22 and 23. Write the letter of the correct answer in the space provided.

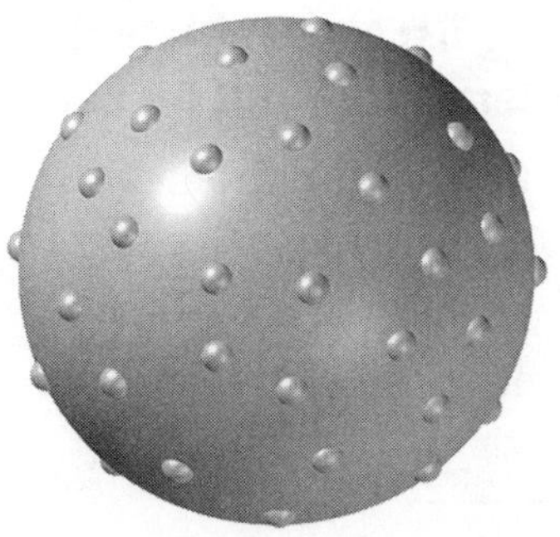

_______**22.** Who proposed this new model of an atom?
    a. Bohr
    b. Thomson
    c. Rutherford
    d. Democritus

_______**23.** The raised surfaces show
    a. protons.
    b. electrons.
    c. neutrons.
    d. isotopes.

Chapter Test B

Introduction to Atoms

USING KEY TERMS

Use the terms from the following list to complete the sentences below. Each term may be used only once. Some terms may not be used.

atom	atomic number	electron
nucleus	atomic mass	electron cloud
proton	isotope	neutron

1. A positively charged particle in the nucleus of an atom is called

a(n) ____________________.

2. An atom of an element that has the same number of protons but different

numbers of neutrons is called a(n) ____________________.

3. The region in an atom that contains most of the mass is called

the ____________________.

4. The number of protons in an atom determines its ____________________.

5. The weighted average of all the naturally occurring isotopes of an element is

called the ____________________.

6. The smallest particle into which an element can be divided and still be the

same substance is a(n) ____________________.

UNDERSTANDING KEY IDEAS

Write the letter of the correct answer in the space provided.

_______ **7.** What did Bohr, Democritus, Thomson, Dalton, and Rutherford all have
in common?
   a. They each identified the electromagnetic force of atoms.
   b. They each identified new electron clouds.
   c. They each developed ideas about atoms.
   d. They each conducted experiments with ions.

❘ Chapter Test B *continued*

_______ **8.** In Thomson's "plum-pudding model" of the atom, the plums represent
    a. atoms.   **c.** neutrons.
    b. protons.   **d.** electrons.

_______ **9.** An atom of carbon with 6 protons, 6 electrons, and 6 neutrons would
have a mass number of
    a. 6.   **c.** 12.
    b. 18.   **d.** 15.

_______ **10.** In an atom, which has the least mass?
    a. nucleus   **c.** neutron
    b. proton   **d.** electron

_______ **11.** If hydrogen-1 has 1 proton, how many protons does hydrogen-2 have?
    a. 2   **c.** 3
    b. 1   **d.** 4

12. How was Bohr's theory of atomic structure similar to the current theory?

____

____

____

____

____

____

13. How was Bohr's theory of atomic structure different from the current theory?

____

____

____

____

____

____

❘ Chapter Test B *continued*

14. Describe the difference between atomic number and atomic mass.

____

____

____

15. How are protons in the nucleus of an atom able to stay close to one another even though they have the same charge?

____

____

____

____

CRITICAL THINKING

16. Long ago, people tried to change inexpensive metals, such as lead, into gold. What fundamental principle of matter did these people fail to understand?

____

____

____

____

17. The ionosphere is a region of Earth's upper atmosphere. From the name ionosphere, what can you conclude about the gases that make up this region?

____

____

____

____

18. The approximate composition of naturally occurring magnesium is as follows: 79% magnesium-24, 10% magnesium-25, and 11% magnesium-26. Calculate the atomic mass of magnesium. Show your work.

| Chapter Test B *continued*

CONCEPT MAPPING

19. Use the following terms to complete the concept map below:

  charges   density   strong force
  neutrons   electromagnetic force

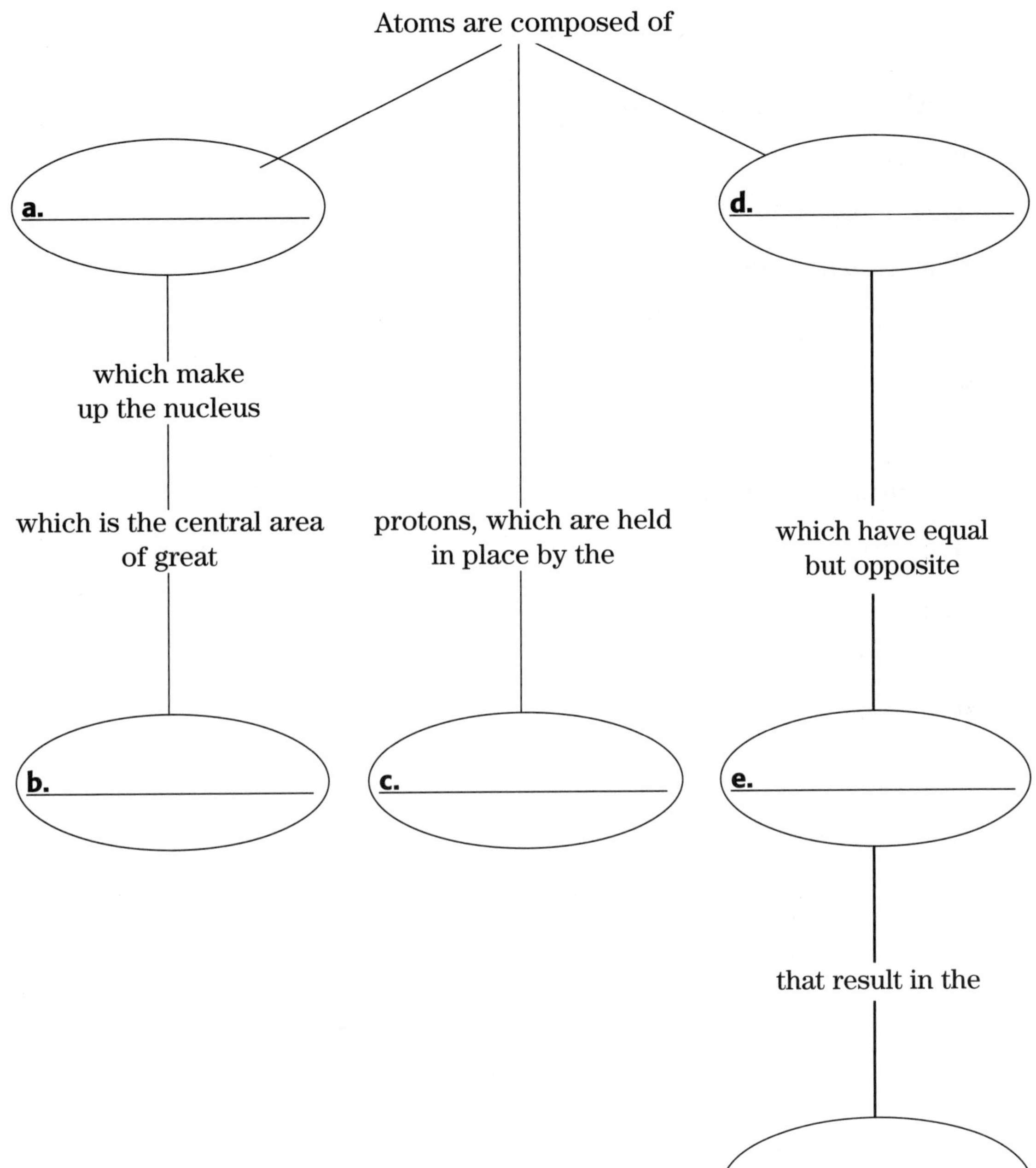

Chapter Test C

Introduction to Atoms
MULTIPLE CHOICE

<u>Circle the letter</u> of the best answer for each question.

1. What was one of Dalton's ideas?

   a. All substances are made of atoms.

   b. Atoms can be divided.

   c. Atoms can be destroyed.

   d. Most substances are made of atoms.

2. What took place in the late 1880s?

   a. Dalton created a new atomic theory.

   b. Dalton disproved his theory.

   c. Dalton's theory was proved.

   d. Dalton's theory was changed.

3. What is the meaning of atom?

   a. "dividable"

   b. "invisible"

   c. "hard particles"

   d. "not able to be divided"

4. Which statement about atoms is true?

   a. A penny has about 20,000 atoms.

   b. Aluminum has large atoms.

   c. A penny has more atoms than Earth has people.

   d. Aluminum has a diameter of about 3 cm.

| Chapter Test C *continued*

MULTIPLE CHOICE
Circle the letter of the best answer for each question.

5. Which statement about isotopes is true?

   a. They have the same number of protons.

   b. They have the same number of neutrons.

   c. They have a different atomic number.

   d. They have the same mass.

6. According to Rutherford, what was in the center of an atom?

   a. an electron

   b. a nucleus

   c. a particle

   d. a proton

7. Which phrase describes radioactive isotopes?

   a. They are stable.

   b. They never change.

   c. They are unstable.

   d. They don't produce energy.

8. Which of the following has the least mass in an atom?

   a. nucleus

   b. proton

   c. neuton

   d. electron

MATCHING

Read the description. Then, <u>draw a line</u> from the dot next to each description to the matching word.

9. positively charged particle ●   **a.** electron

10. negatively charged particle ●   **b.** proton

11. uncharged particle ●   **c.** neutron

---

12. sum of the protons and
neutrons ●

        a. atomic mass unit

13. mass of an atom expressed in ●
atomic mass units
        b. atomic number

14. unit that describes the mass ●
of an atom
        c. mass number

        d. atomic mass

15. number of protons in the ●
nucleus

| Chapter Test C *continued*

FILL-IN-THE BLANK

Read the words in the box. Read the sentences. <u>Fill in each blank</u> with the word or phrase that best completes the sentence.

electrons	electron-cloud	protons
nucleus	atoms	isotopes

16. Thomson discovered the negatively charged particles called

_______________________________.

17. Rutherford believed that each atom has a(n)

_______________________________ at its center.

18. The current atomic theory includes the

_______________________________ model.

19. All substances are made of _______________________________.

20. Isotopes always have the same number of

_______________________________.

21. Most elements have a mixture of two or more

_______________________________.

strong	gravitational	electromagnetic

22. Protons stay together in the nucleus because of

_______________________________ force.

23. Objects are pulled toward one another by

_______________________________ force.

24. Electrons around the nucleus are held in place by

_______________________________ force.

Performance-Based Assessment

OBJECTIVE

Even though we can't see them, electrons are all around us in everything we see and touch. In this activity, you will observe how the charges of electrons interact.

KNOW THE SCORE!

As you work through the activity, keep in mind that you will be earning a grade for the following:

- how well you work with the materials and equipment (20%)
- the quality and clarity of your observations (40%)
- how well you use your observations to answer analysis questions (40%)

Using Scientific Methods

ASK A QUESTION

How do charged objects affect other objects?

MATERIALS AND EQUIPMENT

- two large balloons
- string (1 m)
- water tap
- fluorescent tube

SAFETY INFORMATION 

- Wipe up spills right away
- Don't touch broken fluorescent tubes

PROCEDURE

1. Blow up your balloons and tie them off.

2. Tie one end of the string to each of the balloons. Have the group member with the longest, driest hair rub the two balloons in his or her hair for 20 seconds. Then hold the string in the middle with two fingers.

3. What happens when the balloons are brought together?

____

4. Turn on the water tap partway so the that flow is just a trickle. Recharge one of the balloons with your hair. Hold the balloon next to the water stream.

5. What happens to the stream of water when you bring the balloon near it?

____

| Performance-Based Assessment *continued*

6. Recharge the other balloon. Ask your teacher to dim the lights. Now, holding the tube in the middle, touch the balloon to the fluorescent tube near the tube's end. Describe what happens.

____

ANALYSIS

7. What happened to the charges of the balloons when you rubbed them in your hair?

____

____

8. Based on your observations in Step 2 of the procedure, explain why the two balloons moved as they did.

____

____

9. Based on your observations in Step 4 of the procedure, what can you conclude about the electrical charge of the stream of water?

____

____

10. What do you think caused the reaction in the fluorescent tube?

____

____

11. What does this activity show about the mobility of electrons?

____

____

Standardized Test Preparation

READING

Read each of the passages below. Then, answer the questions that follow each passage.

Passage 1 In the Bohr model of the atom, electrons can be found only in certain energy levels. Electrons "jump" from one level to the next level without passing through any of the regions in between. When an electron moves from one level to another, it gains or loses energy, depending on the direction of its jump. Bohr's model explained an unusual event. When electric charges pass through atoms of a gaseous element, the gas produces a glowing light, like in a neon sign. If this light is passed through a prism, a pattern of lines appears, each line having a different color. The pattern depends on the element—neon has one pattern, and helium has another. In Bohr's model, the lines are caused by electron jumps from higher to lower energy levels. Because only certain jumps are possible, electrons release energy only in certain quantities. These "packets" of energy produce the lines that are seen.

_______ **1.** In the Bohr model of the atom, what limitation is placed on electrons?
   A the number of electrons in an atom
   B the electrons' being found only in certain energy levels
   C the size of electrons
   D the speed of electrons

_______ **2.** What causes the colored lines that appear when the light from a gas is passed through a prism?
   F packets of energy released by electron jumps
   G electrons changing color
   H atoms of the gas exchanging electrons
   I There is not enough information to determine the answer.

Standardized Test Preparation *continued*

Passage 2 No one has ever seen a living dinosaur, but scientists have determined the appearance of *Tyrannosaurus rex* by studying fossilized skeletons. Scientists theorize that these extinct creatures had big hind legs, small front legs, a long, whip-like tail, and a mouth full of dagger-shaped teeth. However, theories of how *T. rex* walked have been harder to develop. For many years, most scientists thought that *T. rex* plodded slowly like a big, lazy lizard. However, after studying well-preserved dinosaur tracks and noticing skeletal similarities between certain dinosaur fossils and living creatures like the ostrich, many scientists now theorize that *T. rex* could turn on the speed. Some scientists estimate that *T. rex* had bursts of speed of 32 km/h (20 mi/h)!

_______ **1.** According to this passage, where does most of what we know about the appearance of *Tyrannosaurus rex* come from?
   A fossilized skeletons
   B dinosaur tracks
   C living organisms such as the ostrich
   D living specimens of T. rex

_______ **2.** How did scientists conclude that *T. rex* could probably move very quickly?
   F They measured the speed at which it could run.
   G They compared fossilized *T. rex* tracks with *T. rex* skeletons.
   H They studied dinosaur tracks and noted similarities between ostrich skeletons and *T. rex* skeletons.
   I They measured the speed at which ostriches could run.

| Standardized Test Preparation *continued*

INTERPRETING GRAPHICS

Use the diagram of the atom below to answer the questions that follow.

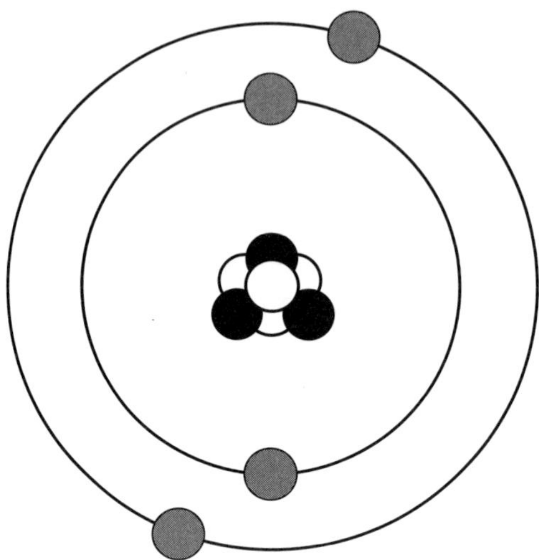

_______ **1.** The black circles in the center of the model represent neutrons. What
do the white circles in the center represent?
A electrons
B protons
C nuclei
D atoms

_______ **2.** What is the mass number of the atom shown in the model?
F 3
G 7
H 9
I 11

_______ **3.** What is the overall charge of the atom shown in the model?
A 12
B 11
C 0
D 21

| Standardized Test Preparation *continued*

MATH

Read each question below, and choose the best answer.

______ **1.** Aimee, Mari, and Brooke are 163 cm, 171 cm, and 175 cm tall. Which of the following measurements is a reasonable average height of these three friends?
  A 170 cm
  B 175 cm
  C 255 cm
  D 509 cm

______ **2.** A certain school has 40 classrooms. Most of the classrooms have 25 to 30 students. Which of the following is a reasonable estimate of the number of students that go to this school?
  F 40 students
  G 100 students
  H 1,100 students
  I 2,000 students

______ **3.** Jenna is setting up a fish tank in her room. The tank is the shape of a rectangular prism. The height of the tank is 38 cm, the width is 23 cm, and the length is 62 cm. The tank is filled with water to a point that is 7 cm from the top. How much water is in the tank?
  A 44,206 cm^3
  B 48,070 cm^3
  C 54,188 cm^3
  D 64,170 cm^3

______ **4.** Which of the following is equal to 8^5?
  F $8 + 8 + 8 + 8 + 8$
  G $5 \times 5 \times 5 \times 5 \times 5 \times 5 \times 5 \times 5$
  H 5×8
  I $8 \times 8 \times 8 \times 8 \times 8$

Model-Making Lab)

Made to Order

Imagine that you are an employee at the Elements-4-U Company, which custom builds elements. Your job is to construct the atomic nucleus for each element ordered by your clients. You were hired for the position because of your knowledge about what a nucleus is made of and your understanding of how isotopes of an element differ from each other. Now, it's time to put that knowledge to work!

OBJECTIVES

Build models of nuclei of certain isotopes.

Use the periodic table to determine the composition of atomic nuclei.

MATERIALS

- periodic table
- plastic-foam balls, blue, 2–3 cm in diameter (6)
- plastic-foam balls, white, 2–3 cm in diameter (4)
- toothpicks (20)

SAFETY

PROCEDURE

1. Use the table below to record your data. Expand the table as needed to include more elements.

Data Collection Table

	Hydrogen-1	Hydrogen-2	Helium-2	Helium-4	Beryllium-9	Beryllium-10
Number of protons						
Number of neutrons						
Atomic number						
Mass number						

2. Your first assignment is the nucleus of hydrogen-1. Pick up one proton (a white plastic-foam ball). Congratulations! You have built a hydrogen-1 nucleus, the simplest nucleus possible.

3. Count the number of protons and neutrons in the nucleus, and fill in rows 1 and 2 for this element in the table.

4. Use the information in rows 1 and 2 to determine the atomic number and mass number of the element. Record this information in the table.

Made to Order *continued*

5. Draw a picture of your model.

6. Hydrogen-2 is an isotope of hydrogen that has one proton and one neutron. Using a strong-force connector, add a neutron to your hydrogen-1 nucleus. (Remember that in a nucleus, the protons and neutrons are held together by the strong force, which is represented in this activity by the toothpicks.) Repeat steps 3–5.

7. Helium-3 is an isotope of helium that has two protons and one neutron. Add one proton to your hydrogen-2 nucleus to create a helium-3 nucleus. Each particle should be connected to the other two particles so that they make a triangle, not a line. Protons and neutrons always form the smallest arrangement possible because the strong force pulls them together. Then, repeat steps 3–5.

8. For the next part of the lab, you will need to use information from the periodic table of the elements. Look at the illustration below. It shows the periodic table entry for carbon. You can find the atomic number of any element at the top of its entry on the periodic table. For example, the atomic number of carbon is 6.

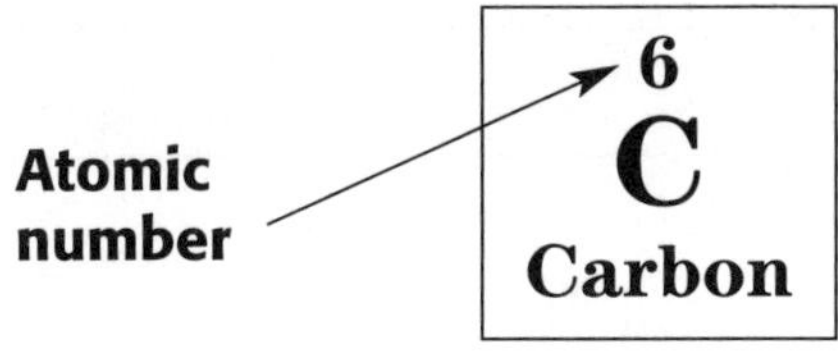

9. Use the information in the periodic table to build models of the following isotopes of elements: helium-4, lithium-7, beryllium-9, and beryllium-10. Remember to put the protons and neutrons as close together as possible— each particle should attach to at least two others. Repeat steps 3–5 for each isotope.

ANALYZE THE RESULTS

1. Examining Data What is the relationship between the number of protons and the atomic number?

____

2. Analyzing Data If you know the atomic number and the mass number of an isotope, how could you figure out the number of neutrons in its nucleus?

____

DRAW CONCLUSIONS

3. Applying Conclusions Look up uranium on the periodic table. What is the atomic number of uranium? How many neutrons does the isotope uranium-235 have?

____

____

4. Evaluating Models Compare your model with the models of your classmates. How are the models similar? How are they different?

____

____

____

APPLYING YOUR DATA

Combine your model with one that another student has made to create a single nucleus. Identify the element (and isotope) you have created.

____

____

Vocabulary Activity

Atomic Anagrams

After you finish reading the chapter, try this puzzle.

Use the definitions below to unscramble the vocabulary words.

1. weighted average of the mass of all naturally occurring isotopes of the same element

   MICTOA SAMS ____

2. the smallest unit of an element that maintains the properties of an element

   MOATS ____

3. positively charged particle in the atom

   TORPNO ____

4. made up of protons and neutrons

   UCSELUN ____

5. particle in the atom that has no charge

   TRONUNE ____

6. atoms with the same number of protons but different numbers of neutrons

   SOOTPIES ____

7. negatively charged particle in the atom

   CLEENROT ____

8. number of protons in a nucleus

   MICOTA BRUMEN ____

9. regions where electrons are likely to be found

   RENECTOL SCUDLO ____

10. SI unit used to express the mass of atomic particles

    TMCOAI SASM NTUI ____

11. sum of protons and neutrons

    SAMS BRUNEM ____

Activity

SciLinks Activity

Introduction to Atoms

Go to www.scilinks.org. To find links related to atoms, type in the keyword HSM0799. Use the links to answer the following questions about the atom.

1. If an electron weighed as much as a dime, how much would a proton weigh?

____

____

2. How do the masses of protons and neutrons compare?

____

____

3. How many naturally occurring kinds of atoms are there?

____

____

4. How many atoms have scientists been able to make in labs?

____

____

5. In 1968, scientists discovered new particles inside the proton. What are these particles? How many of these particles are in each proton?

____

____

6. When did scientists discover the neutron?

____

7. How many quarks are there in each neutron? In each proton?

____

8. What holds quarks together?

____

Performance-Based Assessment

Teacher Notes and Answer Key

Susan Gorman
Northridge Middle School
North Richland Hills, Texas

PURPOSE

Students demonstrate the stripping of electrons from atoms, repulsion of like charges, attraction of opposites, and electron flow.

TIME REQUIRED

One 45-minute class period. Students will need 20 minutes at the activity station and 25 minutes to answer the analysis questions.

RATING

Easy ←——1——2——3——4——→ Hard

Teacher Prep–1
Student Set-Up–1
Concept Level–2
Clean Up–1

ADVANCE PREPARATION

Equip each activity station with the necessary materials. Each activity station should have access to a sink with running water.

SAFETY INFORMATION 

Wipe up spills immediately. Instruct students not to touch broken fluorescent tubes. Have a disposal container for sharps available in case of fluorescent tube breakage.

TEACHING STRATEGIES

This activity works best in groups of 2–3 students. The balloons in the activity are charged by rubbing them on the students' hair. The reaction of the balloon to the students' hair and to the stream of tap water demonstrates the presence of negative and positive charges. The type of charge affects the balloon's reaction to other materials. The reaction between the balloon and the fluorescent tube illustrates the mobility of electrons.

Performance-Based Assessment *continued*

Evaluation Strategies

Use the following rubric to help evaluate student performance.

Rubric for Assessment

Possible points	Appropriate use of materials and equipment (20 points possible)
20–15	Successfully completes activity; safe and careful handling of materials and equipment; attention to detail; superior lab skills
14–10	Task is generally complete; successful use of materials and equipment; sound knowledge of lab techniques; somewhat unfocused performance
9–1	Attempts to complete tasks yield inadequate results; sloppy lab technique; apparent lack of skill
	Quality and clarity of observations (40 points possible)
40–30	Superior observations stated clearly and accurately; high level of detail
29–20	Accurate observations; moderate level of detail; correct use of units of measurement
19–10	Complete observations, but expressed in unclear manner; may include minor inaccuracies; attempts to use units of measurement include errors or inconsistencies
9–1	Erroneous, incomplete, or unclear observations; lack of accuracy, details, units of measurement
	Explanation of observations (40 points possible)
40–25	Clear, detailed explanation shows superior knowledge of subject
24–15	Adequate understanding of concepts with minor difficulty in expression
14–1	Poor understanding of concepts; explanation unclear or not relevant; substantial factual errors

Name _______________________________ Class _______________ Date ___________

Performance-Based Assessment

OBJECTIVE

Even though we can't see them, electrons are all around us in everything we see and touch. In this activity, you will observe how the charges of electrons interact.

KNOW THE SCORE!

As you work through the activity, keep in mind that you will be earning a grade for the following:

- how well you work with the materials and equipment (20%)
- the quality and clarity of your observations (40%)
- how well you use your observations to answer analysis questions (40%)

Using Scientific Methods

ASK A QUESTION

How do charged objects affect other objects?

MATERIALS AND EQUIPMENT

- two large balloons
- string (1 m)
- water tap
- fluorescent tube

SAFETY INFORMATION 

- Wipe up spills right away
- Don't touch broken fluorescent tubes

PROCEDURE

1. Blow up your balloons and tie them off.

2. Tie one end of the string to each of the balloons. Have the group member with the longest, driest hair rub the two balloons in his or her hair for 20 seconds. Then hold the string in the middle with two fingers.

3. What happens when the balloons are brought together?

   The balloons move apart from each other.

4. Turn on the water tap partway so the that flow is just a trickle. Recharge one of the balloons with your hair. Hold the balloon next to the water stream.

5. What happens to the stream of water when you bring the balloon near it?

   The stream of water bends toward the balloon.

Name _______________________________ Class _______________ Date _____________

Performance-Based Assessment *continued*

6. Recharge the other balloon. Ask your teacher to dim the lights. Now, holding the tube in the middle, touch the balloon to the fluorescent tube near the tube's end. Describe what happens.

The balloon causes a flash of light in the fluorescent tube.

ANALYSIS

7. What happened to the charges of the balloons when you rubbed them in your hair?

The balloons picked up electrons from my hair, which gave them a negative

electric charge.

8. Based on your observations in Step 2 of the procedure, explain why the two balloons moved as they did.

Like charges repel each other, and both of the balloons were negatively

charged.

9. Based on your observations in Step 4 of the procedure, what can you conclude about the electrical charge of the stream of water?

The stream of water must have a positive charge because it is attracted to

the negatively charged balloon.

10. What do you think caused the reaction in the fluorescent tube?

The electrons passed very quickly into the fluorescent tube, which caused

the flash of light.

11. What does this activity show about the mobility of electrons?

Electrons can move from place to place; they are not permanently attached

to atoms.

   DATASHEET FOR CHAPTER LAB

Made to Order

Teacher Notes and Answer Key

TIME REQUIRED

One 45-minute class period

LAB RATINGS

Easy ← 1   2   3   4 → Hard

Teacher Prep–2
Student Set-Up–1
Concept Level–3
Clean Up–1

MATERIALS

The supplies listed are for a pair of students. Foam balls of any color are.
acceptable as long as there are two colors. Flexible pipe cleaners may be used
instead of toothpicks.

SAFETY CAUTION

• Remind students to review all safety cautions and icons before beginning this
  lab activity.

PREPARATION NOTES

Before you begin this lab, review the concepts of isotopes, atomic number, and
mass number. To create colored balls, use colored markers or spray paint.
Alternatively, you can label white balls with "N" or "P." If you prefer to make two-
dimensional models, use colored dots (from an office-supply store) to represent
the different particles. Reinforce the idea that the particles should be compact—
the strong force binds the particles together as tightly as possible.

Name _______________________________ Class _______________ Date _____________

<table>
<tr><td>Model-Making Lab)</td><td>**DATASHEET FOR CHAPTER LAB**</td></tr>
</table>

Made to Order

Imagine that you are an employee at the Elements-4-U Company, which custom builds elements. Your job is to construct the atomic nucleus for each element ordered by your clients. You were hired for the position because of your knowledge about what a nucleus is made of and your understanding of how isotopes of an element differ from each other. Now, it's time to put that knowledge to work!

OBJECTIVES

Build models of nuclei of certain isotopes.

Use the periodic table to determine the composition of atomic nuclei.

MATERIALS

- periodic table
- plastic-foam balls, blue, 2–3 cm in diameter (6)
- plastic-foam balls, white, 2–3 cm in diameter (4)
- toothpicks (20)

SAFETY 

PROCEDURE

1. Use the table below to record your data. Expand the table as needed to include more elements.

Data Collection Table

	Hydrogen-1	Hydrogen-2	Helium-2	Helium-4	Beryllium-9	Beryllium-10
Number of protons						
Number of neutrons						
Atomic number						
Mass number						

2. Your first assignment is the nucleus of hydrogen-1. Pick up one proton (a white plastic-foam ball). Congratulations! You have built a hydrogen-1 nucleus, the simplest nucleus possible.

3. Count the number of protons and neutrons in the nucleus, and fill in rows 1 and 2 for this element in the table.

4. Use the information in rows 1 and 2 to determine the atomic number and mass number of the element. Record this information in the table.

Name _______________________________ Class _______________ Date _____________

Made to Order *continued*

5. Draw a picture of your model.

6. Hydrogen-2 is an isotope of hydrogen that has one proton and one neutron. Using a strong-force connector, add a neutron to your hydrogen-1 nucleus. (Remember that in a nucleus, the protons and neutrons are held together by the strong force, which is represented in this activity by the toothpicks.) Repeat steps 3–5.

7. Helium-3 is an isotope of helium that has two protons and one neutron. Add one proton to your hydrogen-2 nucleus to create a helium-3 nucleus. Each particle should be connected to the other two particles so that they make a triangle, not a line. Protons and neutrons always form the smallest arrangement possible because the strong force pulls them together. Then, repeat steps 3–5.

8. For the next part of the lab, you will need to use information from the periodic table of the elements. Look at the illustration below. It shows the periodic table entry for carbon. You can find the atomic number of any element at the top of its entry on the periodic table. For example, the atomic number of carbon is 6.

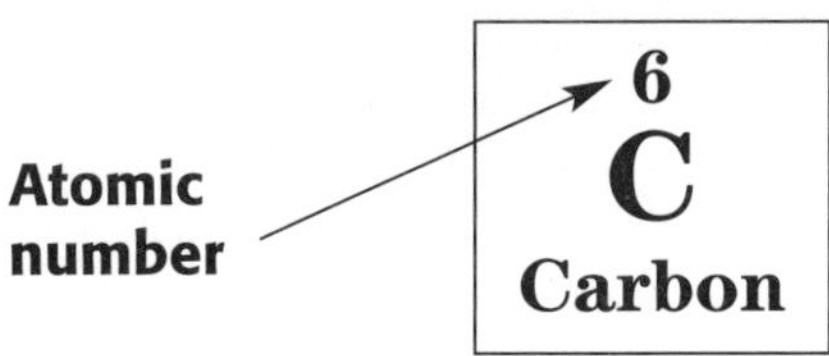

9. Use the information in the periodic table to build models of the following isotopes of elements: helium-4, lithium-7, beryllium-9, and beryllium-10. Remember to put the protons and neutrons as close together as possible— each particle should attach to at least two others. Repeat steps 3–5 for each isotope.

Name _______________________________ Class _______________ Date _______________

Made to Order *continued*

ANALYZE THE RESULTS

1. Examining Data What is the relationship between the number of protons and the atomic number?

The number of protons is the same as the atomic number.

2. Analyzing Data If you know the atomic number and the mass number of an isotope, how could you figure out the number of neutrons in its nucleus?

The number of neutrons equals the mass number minus the atomic number.

DRAW CONCLUSIONS

3. Applying Conclusions Look up uranium on the periodic table. What is the atomic number of uranium? How many neutrons does the isotope uranium-235 have?

a. 92

b. 143 neutrons (235 − 92 = 143)

4. Evaluating Models Compare your model with the models of your classmates. How are the models similar? How are they different?

Sample answer: They differ in the way the protons and neutrons are

connected to each other. They are the same in the number of protons and

neutrons that each of the same isotope has, however.

APPLYING YOUR DATA

Combine your model with one that another student has made to create a single nucleus. Identify the element (and isotope) you have created.

If all of the protons and neutrons are used, the isotope created will be

oxygen-20.

Answer Key

Directed Reading A

SECTION: DEVELOPMENT OF THE ATOMIC THEORY

1. D
2. C
3. Aristotle disagreed with Democritus. At the time, Aristotle had more influence on what people thought than Democritus did. Consequently, people believed Aristotle.
4. atom
5. C
6. Dalton's results suggested that elements combine in specific proportions because they are made of single atoms.
7. positively, negative
8. electrons
9. atom
10. A
11. Most of the particles passed right through the gold foil, some of the particles were deflected, and some of the particles bounced straight back.
12. D
13. nucleus
14. Electron clouds are regions inside the atom where electrons are likely to be found.

SECTION: THE ATOM

1. B
2. F
3. D
4. E
5. A
6. C
7. B
8. hydrogen, proton, electron (no particular order for *proton* and *electron*)
9. nucleus
10. helium
11. protons and neutrons (either order)
12. protons
13. A
14. B
15. B
16. C
17. isotopes

18. atomic mass
19. C
20. A
21. D
22. B

Directed Reading B

SECTION: DEVELOPMENT OF ATOMIC THEORY

1. D
2. C
3. C
4. A
5. D
6. cathode-ray tube
7. positively
8. particles
9. electrons
10. A
11. A
12. B
13. A
14. B
15. A
16. D
17. A

SECTION: THE ATOM

1. B
2. D
3. C
4. A
5. B
6. hydrogen, electron
7. helium
8. neutrons
9. atomic number
10. atomic mass unit
11. A
12. B
13. C
14. B
15. C
16. mass number
17. atomic mass
18. strong force
19. gravitational force
20. weak force
21. electromagnetic force

Vocabulary and Section Summary

SECTION: DEVELOPMENT OF THE ATOMIC THEORY

1. atom: the smallest unit of an element that maintains the properties of an element
2. electron: a subatomic particle that has a negative charge
3. nucleus: in physical science, an atom's central region, which is made up of protons and neutrons
4. electron cloud: a region around the nucleus of an atom where electrons are likely to be found

SECTION: THE ATOM

1. proton: a subatomic particle that has a positive charge and that is found in the nucleus of an atom
2. atomic mass unit: a unit of mass that describes the mass of an atom or molecule
3. neutron: a subatomic particle that has no charge and that is found in the nucleus of an atom
4. atomic number: the number of protons in the nucleus of an atom; the atomic number is the same for all atoms of an element
5. isotope: an atom that has the same number of protons (or the same atomic number) as other atoms of the same element do but that has a different number of neutrons (and thus a different atomic mass)
6. mass number: the sum of the numbers of protons and neutrons in the nucleus of an atom
7. atomic mass: the mass of an atom expressed in atomic mass units

Section Review

SECTION: DEVELOPMENT OF THE ATOMIC THEORY

1. Sample answer: the smallest part of an element that has the properties of that element
2. electron
3. nucleus
4. B
5. He performed experiments and drew conclusions from them to develop his theory.
6. Rutherford's gold foil experiment, in which he observed that most of the positively charged particles he aimed at a piece of gold foil went straight through
7. Bohr suggested that electrons could only move around the nucleus in certain paths. They could jump between these paths, but not stay between them.
8. Bohr's theory held that electrons can only travel in certain paths around the nucleus. The current atomic theory is that electrons travel in regions where they are *likely* to be found.
9. Rutherford placed a surface behind the gold foil, which would glow where the positively charged particles hit it. This shows that he was trying to find out where the particles went after hitting the gold foil.
10. that electrons are mixed throughout an atom

SECTION: THE ATOM

1. Sample answer: Different isotopes have the same number of protons, but different numbers of neutrons.
2. atomic number
3. atomic mass
4. B
5. Gravitational force acts between objects based on their mass. Electromagnetic force attracts objects of opposite electric charge, and repels objects of the same electric charge. The strong force holds the protons and neutrons of atomic nuclei together. The weak force plays a role in radioactive decay.
6. $(0.30 \times 203 \text{ amu}) + (0.70 \times 205 \text{ amu}) = 204.4 \text{ amu}$
7. Because the masses of nuclear particles are so small.
8. No; without neutrons, two protons brought into close contact would repel each other.
9. The two atoms shown are different elements; they have different numbers of protons.

Chapter Review

1. Protons
2. protons
3. Neutrons
4. mass number
5. atomic mass
6. C
7. A
8. D
9. A
10. B
11. electromagnetic force
12. Sample answer: The plum-pudding model describes the atom as a lump of positively charged material with negatively charged particles throughout. The positively charged material is like the pudding, and electrons are like plums in it.
13. $(0.60 \times 69 \text{ amu}) + (0.40 \times 71 \text{ amu}) = 69.8 \text{ amu}$
14. number of protons = atomic number = 40
number of neutrons = mass number–atomic number = 50
number of electrons = number of protons = 40
15. An answer to this exercise can be found at the end of the teacher edition.
16. Scientists must determine the atomic number, or the number of protons, in the newly formed nucleus. The nucleus is that of a new element only if the number of protons is different from all known elements.
17. Sample answer: Dalton's atomic theory was the first one based on experimental evidence. It helps show how a theory develops as new information is discovered.
18. No; the results of an experiment must be repeatable to be considered valid.
19. A and C
20. 3
21. 7

Reinforcement

A. Rutherford, 1909–1911
B. Rutherford, 1909–1911
C. Thomson, 1897
D. Bohr, 1913
E. Dalton, 1803
F. Thomson, 1897
G. Democritus, 440 BCE
H. Rutherford, 1909–1911
I. Democritus, 440 BCE
J. Dalton, 1803
K. Bohr, 1913
L. Schrödinger and Heisenberg, twentieth century
M. Thomson, 1897
N. Rutherford, 1909–1911
O. Dalton, 1803
P. Schrödinger and Heisenberg, twentieth century
Q. Dalton, 1803
R. Democritus, 440 BCE
S. Rutherford, 1909–1911
T. Dalton, 1803

Critical Thinking

1. Because the nucleus is positively charged, the suit also must have been positively charged to create this repulsion.
2. Her suit would have had a neutral charge.
3. Answers will vary according to the forces students discuss. Sample answer: If her suit was positively charged, then the electromagnetic force would pull her toward the electrons in the atom.
4. Knowing that the atomic number of carbon is six, Professor Pending could look for an atom with six protons in its nucleus.
5. An atom's mass number is equal to its protons plus its neutrons. All carbon atoms have six protons. Carbon-14 would have six protons and eight neutrons. Professor Pending could use this characteristic to identify the correct atom.
6. A negatively charged ion has more electrons than protons. Therefore, the ion would require at least seven electrons.

7. The orbit of the moon can be compared with the movement of an electron. They both travel around objects with greater masses. They differ with respect to the forces that cause their motion. The moon orbits Earth because of gravity. The motion of an electron around a nucleus is a result of electromagnetism.

Section Quizzes

SECTION: DEVELOPMENT OF THE ATOMIC THEORY

1. C
2. B
3. A
4. B
5. A

SECTION: THE ATOM

1. D
2. I
3. C
4. B
5. J
6. E
7. H
8. A
9. G
10. F

Chapter Test A

1. C
2. D
3. C
4. D
5. A
6. C
7. D
8. G
9. H
10. B
11. C
12. F
13. J
14. I
15. A
16. E
17. D
18. A
19. D
20. B
21. C

22. B
23. B

Chapter Test B

1. proton
2. isotope
3. nucleus
4. atomic number
5. atomic mass
6. atom
7. C
8. D
9. C
10. D
11. B
12. Bohr's theory and the current theory both have electrons traveling in orbits around a central nucleus.
13. In Bohr's theory, the electrons move only in definite paths. Current atomic theory expresses the position of electrons in terms of the probability that electrons will be found in regions of the atom called electron clouds.
14. The atomic number is the number of protons in an atom. Atomic mass is the sum of the number of protons and neutrons in an atom of a particular isotope.
15. Protons can stay close to one another inside the nucleus of an atom due to the strong force. Although the electromagnetic force causes particles with the same charge to repel each other, the strong force is greater than the electromagnetic force at close distances.
16. These people did not understand that elements, such as lead and gold, are divided into smaller particles called atoms. Each atom of an element is composed of a unique number of protons, neutrons, and electrons. Atoms cannot be created or destroyed. Therefore, it is not possible to simply convert one metal into another.
17. The ionosphere must contain ions, which are electrically charged particles. To be charged, the numbers of electrons and protons in the particles must not be equal.
18. $(0.79 \times 24) + (0.10 \times 25) + (0.11 \times 26) = 24.32$ amu

CONCEPT MAPPING

19. a. neutrons, **b.** density, **c.** strong force,
d. electrons, **e.** charges,
f. electromagnetic force

Chapter Test C

1. A
2. D
3. D
4. C
5. A
6. B
7. C
8. D
9. B
10. A
11. C
12. C
13. D
14. A
15. B
16. electrons
17. nucleus
18. electron-cloud
19. atoms
20. protons
21. isotopes
22. strong
23. gravitational
24. electromagnetic

Standardized Test Preparation

READING

Passage 1
  1. B
  2. F

Passage 2
  1. A
  2. H

INTERPRETING GRAPHICS

  1. B
  2. G
  3. D

MATH

  1. B
  2. H
  3. A
  4. I

Vocabulary Activity

1. atomic mass
2. atoms
3. proton
4. nucleus
5. neutron
6. isotopes
7. electron
8. atomic number
9. electron clouds
10. atomic mass unit
11. mass number

SciLinks Activity

1. It would weigh as much as a gallon of milk.
2. The masses are almost the same.
3. 90
4. about 25
5. quarks, three
6. 1932
7. three in each neutron and proton
8. Particles called gluons hold quarks together.

Lesson Plan

Section: Development of the Atomic Theory

Pacing

Regular Schedule   **with lab(s):** N/A   **without lab(s):** 1 day

Block Schedule: **with lab(s):** N/A   **without lab(s):** 0.5 day

Objectives

1. Describe some of the experiments that led to the current atomic theory.

2. Compare the different models of the atom.

3. Explain how the atomic theory has changed as scientists have discovered new information about the atom.

National Science Education Standards Covered

UCP 2: Evidence, models, and explanation

SAI 2: Understandings about scientific inquiry

HNS 1: Science as a human endeavor

HNS 2: Nature of science

HNS 3: History of science

KEY

SE = Student Edition   TE = Teacher's Edition

CRF = Chapter Resource File

FOCUS *(5 minutes)*

_ **Chapter Starter Transparency** Use this transparency to introduce the chapter.

_ **Bellringer, TE** Have students write what they think a statement by Democritus means.

_ **Bellringer Transparency** Use this transparency as students enter the classroom and find their seats.

_ **Reading Strategy, SE** Have students create an outline of the section, using section headings.

MOTIVATE *(10 minutes)*

_ **Activity, Photographic Dots, TE** Have students use a magnifying lens to examine newspaper photographs. (**GENERAL**)

TEACH *(20 minutes)*

_ **Reading Strategy, Making a Prediction, TE** Ask students to predict whether Democritus's theory is correct or even partly correct. (**GENERAL**)

- **Discussion, Dalton Discussion, TE** Using diagrams, discuss how Dalton's atomic theory explains his observations. (**GENERAL**)

- **Group Activity, Scientist Flashcards, TE** Have students create flash cards that connect the scientists in this section with their accomplishments. (**BASIC**)

- **Activity, Static Electricity, TE** Have students complete a static electricity activity. (**GENERAL**)

- **Discussion, Influences on Atomic Theory, TE** Have students write a paragraph about the person they believe had the greatest impact on present-day atomic theory. (**GENERAL**)

- **Connection Activity Literature, The Shrinking Man, TE** Read excerpts of *The Shrinking Man* to students. (**GENERAL**)

- **Directed Reading A/B, CRF** These worksheets reinforce basic concepts and vocabulary presented in the lesson. (**BASIC/SPECIAL NEEDS**)

- **Vocabulary and Section Summary, CRF** Students write definitions of key terms and read a summary of section content. (**GENERAL**)

- **Reinforcement, CRF** This worksheet reinforces key concepts in the chapter. (**GENERAL**)

- **SciLinks Activity, Inside the Atom, SciLinks code HSM0799, CRF** Students research Internet resources related to atoms. (**GENERAL**)

- **Teaching Transparency, Thomson's Cathode-Ray Tube Experiment** Use this graphic to help students understand the experiment that led to the discovery of electrons.

- **Teaching Transparency, Rutherford's Gold-Foil Experiment** Use this graphic to help students understand the experiment that led to Rutherford's revision of the atomic theory.

CLOSE *(10 minutes)*

- **Reteaching, Table of Atomic Discoveries, TE** Construct a table that summarizes the discoveries of the scientists covered in this section. (**BASIC**)

- **Homework, Theories of Atomic Structure, TE** Have students write a paragraph explaining why making and using models of scientific discoveries are important. (**GENERAL**)

- **Section Review, SE** Students answer end-of-section vocabulary, key ideas, and critical thinking, and interpreting graphics questions. (**GENERAL**)

- **Section Quiz, CRF** Students answer 5 objective questions about atoms. (**GENERAL**)

- **Quiz, TE** Students answer 3 questions about atoms. (**GENERAL**)

- **Alternative Assessment, TE** Students role-play scientists or philosophers discussed in this section. (**GENERAL**)

Lesson Plan

Section: The Atom

Pacing

Regular Schedule   **with lab(s):** 2 days   **without lab(s):** 1 day

Block Schedule: **with lab(s):** 1 days   **without lab(s):** 0.5 day

Objectives

1. Describe the size of an atom.

2. Name the parts of an atom.

3. Describe the relationship between numbers of protons and neutrons and atomic number.

4. State how isotopes differ.

5. Calculate atomic masses.

6. Describe the forces within an atom.

National Science Education Standards Covered

PS 1c: Chemical elements do not break down during normal laboratory reactions involving such treatments as heating, exposure to electric current, or reaction with acids. There are more than 100 known elements that combine in a multitude of ways to produce compounds, which account for the living and nonliving substances that we encounter.

KEY

SE = Student Edition   **TE** = Teacher's Edition

CRF = Chapter Resource File

FOCUS *(5 minutes)*

_ **Bellringer, TE** Ask students if they believe the definition of the atom is still correct in light of the discovery of particles that are smaller than atoms.

_ **Bellringer Transparency** Use this transparency as students enter the classroom and find their seats.

_ **Reading Strategy, SE** Have students create a concept map, using important terms from the section.

MOTIVATE *(10 minutes)*

_ **Discussion, The Atomic Scale, TE** Discuss the number of atoms in a penny. (**GENERAL**)

TEACH *(65 minutes)*

_ **Activity, TE** Have advanced learners research the contributions of Japanese scientists. (**ADVANCED**)

_ **Connection Activity, Math, TE** Have students determine how many gold atoms it would take to measure the width of a dollar bill. (**GENERAL**)

_ **Connection to Earth Science, TE** Show students the arrangement of gold atoms in a sample of gold. (**GENERAL**)

_ **Connection Activity, Math, TE** Have students calculate the diameter of an atom that has a nucleus the size of a penny. (**GENERAL**)

_ **Connection Activity, Real World, TE** Tell students about the development of the Atomic Energy Commission. (**GENERAL**)

_ **Reading Strategy, Atomic Diagrams, TE** Have students create and label diagrams of several different atoms in their science journals. (**GENERAL**)

_ **Guided Practice, Atomic Numbers and the Elements, TE** Have students use the periodic table to find the atomic numbers of different elements. (**GENERAL**)

_ **Connection to Paleontology, TE** Tell students about carbon dating. (**GENERAL**)

_ **Chapter Lab, Made to Order, SE** Students build models of nuclei of certain isotopes and use the periodic table.

_ **Directed Reading A/B, CRF** These worksheets reinforce basic concepts and vocabulary presented in the lesson. (**BASIC/SPECIAL NEEDS**)

_ **Vocabulary and Section Summary, CRF** Students write definitions of key terms and read a summary of section content. (**GENERAL**)

_ **Critical Thinking, CRF** Ask students to fill out the worksheet about the incredible shrinking scientist. (**ADVANCED**)

CLOSE *(10 minutes)*

_ **Reteaching, Descriptions of Atomic Structure, TE** Have students write a simple description of an atom. (**BASIC**)

_ **Section Review, SE** Students answer end-of-section vocabulary, key ideas, math, critical thinking, and interpreting graphics questions. (**GENERAL**)

_ **Section Quiz, CRF** Students answer 10 objective questions about atoms. (**GENERAL**)

_ **Quiz, TE** Students answer 3 questions about atoms. (**GENERAL**)

_ **Alternative Assessment, TE** Students create a concept map using key terms from the section. (**GENERAL**)

Lesson Plan

End of Chapter Review and Assessment

Pacing

Regular Schedule   **with lab(s):** N/A   **without lab(s):** 2 days

Block Schedule: **with lab(s):** N/A   **without lab(s):** 1 day

---

KEY

SE = Student Edition   **TE** = Teacher's Edition

CRF = Chapter Resource File

_ **Chapter Review, SE** Students answer end-of-chapter vocabulary, key ideas, critical thinking, and graphics questions. (**GENERAL**)

_ **Vocabulary Activity, CRF** Students review vocabulary terms by completing an atomic anagram activity. (**GENERAL**)

_ **Concept Mapping Transparency** Use this graphic to help students review key concepts.

_ **Chapter Test A/B/C, CRF** Assign questions from the appropriate test for chapter assessment. (**GENERAL/ADVANCED/SPECIAL NEEDS**)

_ **Standardized Test Preparation, SE** Students answer reading comprehension, math, and interpreting graphics questions in the format of a standardized test. (**GENERAL**)

_ **Test Generator, One-Stop Planner.** Create a customized homework assignment, quiz, or test using the HRW Test Generator program. (**GENERAL**)

Introduction to Atoms

MULTIPLE CHOICE

1. The smallest particle into which an element can be divided and still be the same substance is called a(n)
   a. nucleus.
   b. electron.
   c. atom.
   d. neutron.
   Answer: C   Difficulty: 1   Section: 1   Objective: 3

2. What particle did J. J. Thomson discover?
   a. neutron
   b. electron
   c. atom
   d. proton
   Answer: B   Difficulty: 1   Section: 1   Objective: 1

3. How would you describe the nucleus?
   a. dense, positively charged
   b. large, positively charged
   c. tiny, negatively charged
   d. dense, negatively charged
   Answer: A   Difficulty: 1   Section: 1   Objective: 2

4. Where are electrons likely to be found?
   a. the nucleus
   b. electron clouds
   c. mixed throughout an atom
   d. paths, or energy levels
   Answer: B   Difficulty: 1   Section: 1   Objective: 3

5. Dalton believed that
   a. atoms of the same element are exactly alike.
   b. most substances are made of atoms.
   c. atoms of different elements are the same.
   d. atoms can be divided.
   Answer: A   Difficulty: 1   Section: 1   Objective: 2

6. What did Democritus, Dalton, Thomson, Rutherford, and Bohr all have in common?
   a. They each identified new elements.
   b. They each identified new isotopes of atoms.
   c. They each contributed to the development of the atomic theory.
   d. They each conducted experiments in which particles collided.
   Answer: C   Difficulty: 1   Section: 1   Objective: 3

7. In Thomson's "plum-pudding" model of the atom, the plums represent
   a. atoms.
   b. protons.
   c. neutrons.
   d. electrons.
   Answer: D   Difficulty: 1   Section: a1   Objective: 3

8. An atom of gold with 79 protons, 79 electrons, and 118 neutrons would have a mass number of
   a. 39.
   b. 158.
   c. 197.
   d. 276.
   Answer: C   Difficulty: 1   Section: 2   Objective: 5

9. Which of the following has the least mass?
   a. nucleus
   b. proton
   c. neutron
   d. electron
   Answer: D   Difficulty: 1   Section: 2   Objective: 1

10. If an isotope of uranium, uranium-235, has 92 protons, how many protons does uranium-238 have?
    a. 92
    b. 95
    c. 143
    d. 146

    Answer: A   Difficulty: 2   Section: 2   Objective: 4

11. How did Democritus describe atoms?
    a. large, soft particles
    b. dividable particles
    c. small, hard particles
    d. a single material with one shape and size

    Answer: C   Difficulty: 1   Section: 1   Objective: 3

12. What is the smallest particle into which an element can be divided and still be the same substance?
    a. electron
    b. neutron
    c. proton
    d. atom

    Answer: D   Difficulty: 1   Section: 1   Objective: 1

13. What did Bohr, Democritus, Thomson, Dalton, and Rutherford all have in common?
    a. They each identified the electromagnetic force of atoms.
    b. They each identified new electron clouds.
    c. They each developed ideas about atoms.
    d. They each conducted experiments with ions.

    Answer: C   Difficulty: 1   Section: 1   Objective: 3

14. In Thomson's "plum-pudding model" of the atom, the plums represent
    a. atoms.
    b. protons.
    c. neutrons.
    d. electrons.

    Answer: D   Difficulty: 1   Section: b1   Objective: 2

15. An atom of carbon with 6 protons, 6 electrons, and 6 neutrons would have a mass number of
    a. 6.
    b. 18.
    c. 12.
    d. 15.

    Answer: C   Difficulty: 2   Section: 2   Objective: 5

16. In an atom, which has the least mass?
    a. nucleus
    b. proton
    c. neutron
    d. electron

    Answer: D   Difficulty: 1   Section: 2   Objective: 1

17. If hydrogen-1 has 1 proton, how many protons does hydrogen-2 have?
    a. 2
    b. 1
    c. 3
    d. 4

    Answer: B   Difficulty: 2   Section: 2   Objective: 4

18. What was one of Dalton's ideas?
    a. All substances are made of atoms.
    b. Atoms can be divided.
    c. Atoms can be destroyed.
    d. Most substances are made of atoms.

    Answer: A   Difficulty: 1   Section: 1   Objective: 2

19. What took place in the late 1880s?
    a. Dalton created a new atomic theory.
    b. Dalton disproved his theory.
    c. Dalton's theory was proved.
    d. Dalton's theory was changed.

    Answer: D   Difficulty: 1   Section: 1   Objective: 3

20. What is the meaning of atom?
    a. "dividable"
    b. "invisible"
    c. "hard particles"
    d. "not able to be divided"

    Answer: D   Difficulty: 1   Section: 1   Objective: 3

21. Which statement about atoms is true?
    a. A penny has about 20,000 atoms.
    b. Aluminum has large atoms.
    c. A penny has more atoms than Earth has people.
    d. Aluminum has a diameter of about 3 cm.
    Answer: C   Difficulty: 1   Section: 2   Objective: 1

22. Which statement about isotopes is true?
    a. They have the same number of protons.
    b. They have the same number of neutrons.
    c. They have a different atomic number.
    d. They have the same mass.
    Answer: A   Difficulty: 1   Section: 2   Objective: 4

23. According to Rutherford, what was in the center of an atom?
    a. an electron   c. a particle
    b. a nucleus   d. a proton
    Answer: D   Difficulty: 1   Section: 1   Objective: 2

24. Which phrase describes radioactive isotopes?
    a. They are stable.   c. They are unstable.
    b. They never change   d. They don't produce energy..
    Answer: C   Difficulty: 1   Section: 2   Objective: 4

25. Which of the following has the least mass in an atom?
    a. nucleus   c. neuton
    b. proton   d. electron
    Answer: D   Difficulty: 1   Section: c2   Objective: 1

COMPLETION

Use the terms from the following list to complete the sentences below.

        atom   atomic number
        nucleus   atomic mass
        proton   isotope
        electron   electron cloud
        neutron

26. A positively charged particle in the nucleus of an atom is called a(n)

    __________________.

    Answer: proton   Difficulty: 1   Section: 2   Objective: 2

27. An atom of an element that has the same number of protons but different numbers of
    neutrons is called a(n) __________________.
    Answer: isotope   Difficulty: 1   Section: 2   Objective: 4

28. The region in an atom that contains most of the mass is called __________________.
    Answer: nucleus   Difficulty: 1   Section: 1   Objective: 2

29. The number of protons in an atom determines its __________________.
    Answer: atomic number
                            Difficulty: 1   Section: 2   Objective: 3

30. The weighted average of all the naturally occurring isotopes of an element is called the

    __________________.

    Answer: atomic mass
                            Difficulty: 1   Section: 2   Objective: 5

31. The smallest particle into which an element can be divided and still be the same substance is a(n) _______________.
    Answer: atom   Difficulty: 1   Section: 1   Objective: 1

Use the terms from the following list to complete the sentences below.

electrons   electron-cloud
nucleus   atoms
isotopes   protons

32. Thomson discovered the negatively charged particles called _______________.
    Answer: electrons   Difficulty: 1   Section: 1   Objective: 3

33. Rutherford believed that each atom has a(n) _______________ at its center.
    Answer: nucleus   Difficulty: 1   Section: 1   Objective: 3

34. The current atomic theory includes the _______________ model.
    Answer: electron cloud
                      Difficulty: 1   Section: c1   Objective: 2

35. All substances are made of _______________.
    Answer: atoms   Difficulty: 1   Section: 1   Objective: 1

36. Isotopes always have the same number of _______________.
    Answer: protons   Difficulty: 1   Section: 2   Objective: 4

37. Most elements have a mixture of two or more _______________.
    Answer: isotopes   Difficulty: 1   Section: 2   Objective: 4

Use the terms from the following list to complete the sentences below.

strong   electromagnetic
gravitational

38. Protons stay together in the nucleus because of _______________ force.
    Answer: strong   Difficulty: 1   Section: 2   Objective: 6

39. Objects are pulled toward one another by _______________ force.
    Answer: gravitational
                      Difficulty: 1   Section: 2   Objective: 6

40. Electrons around the nucleus are held in place by _______________ force.
    Answer: electromagnetic
                      Difficulty: 1   Section: 2   Objective: 6

electrons   forces
atoms   electron clouds
isotopes   neutrons
protons

41. In 1803 John Dalton proposed that all substance are made of _______________.
    Answer: atoms   Difficulty: 1   Section: 1   Objective: 3

42. In 1897 the British scientist J. J. Thomson discovered _______________, the negatively charged particles in the atom.
    Answer: electrons   Difficulty: 1   Section: 1   Objective: 1

43. Twentieth-century scientists believe electrons are found in regions called _______________.
    Answer: electron clouds
                      Difficulty: 1   Section: 1   Objective: 3

44. Neutrons and _____________________ each have a mass of about 1 amu.
    Answer: protons   Difficulty: 1   Section: 2   Objective: 1

45. The pushes and pulls between objects are called _____________________.
    Answer: forces   Difficulty: 1   Section: 2   Objective: 6

46. Because their mass is so small, _____________________ are not included in an atom's mass number.
    Answer: electrons   Difficulty: 1   Section: 2   Objective: 5

47. Isotopes have different numbers of _____________________.
    Answer: neutrons   Difficulty: 1   Section: 2   Objective: 4

48. Atoms that are _____________________ of each other are always the same element.
    Answer: isotopes   Difficulty: 1   Section: 2   Objective: 4

49. A charged particle is called a (an) _____________________.
    Answer: ion   Difficulty: 1   Section: 2   Objective: 3

> nucleus   atom
> mass number   atomic
> number   ion

50. The sum of the protons and neutrons in an atom is called the _____________________.
    Answer: mass number
                      Difficulty: 1   Section: 2   Objective: 5

51. Around 440 BCE, Democritus proposed the idea of a (an) _____________________, a particle that could not be cut in half.
    Answer: atom   Difficulty: 1   Section: 1   Objective: 3

52. In 1911 Ernest Rutherford proposed that each atom has a (an) _____________________, a tiny, extremely dense, positively charged region.
    Answer: nucleus   Difficulty: 1   Section: 1   Objective: 1

53. Most of the atom's mass is found in the _____________________.
    Answer: nucleus   Difficulty: 1   Section: 2   Objective: 2

54. All atoms of an element have the same _____________________.
    Answer: atomic number
                      Difficulty: 1   Section: 2   Objective: 3

55. A hydrogen atom with one proton in its nucleus has a (an) _____________________ of one.
    Answer: atomic number
                      Difficulty: 1   Section: 2   Objective: 3

SHORT ANSWER

56. How was Bohr's theory of atomic structure similar to the current theory?
    Answer:
    Bohr's theory and the current theory both have electrons traveling in orbits around a central nucleus.
    Difficulty: 1   Section: 1   Objective: 2

57. How was Bohr's theory of atomic structure different form the current theory?
    Answer:
    In Bohr's theory, the electrons move only in definite paths. Current atomic theory expresses the position of electrons in terms of the probability that electrons will be found in regions of the atom called electron clouds.
    Difficulty: 1   Section: 1   Objective: 2

58. Describe the difference between atomic number and atomic mass.
    Answer:
    The atomic number is the number of protons in an atom. Atomic mass is the sum of the number of protons and neutrons in an atom of a particular isotope.
    Difficulty: 2   Section: 2   Objective: 3, 5

59. How are protons in the nucleus of an atom able to stay close to one another even though they have the same charge?
    Answer:
    Protons can stay close to one another inside the nucleus of an atom due to the strong force. Although the electromagnetic force causes particles with the same charge to repel each other, the strong force is greater than the electromagnetic force at close distances.
    Difficulty: 1   Section: 2   Objective: 6

60. Compare protons and neutrons.
    Answer:
    Protons are positively charged particles in the nucleus of an atom. Neutrons are particles in the nucleus of an atom that have no charge.
    Difficulty: 2   Section: 2   Objective: 2

61. Put the following atomic models in the proper sequence: Rutherford's model, electron-cloud model, "plum-pudding" model, Bohr's model.
    Answer:
    "plum-pudding" model, Rutherford's model, Bohr's model, electron-cloud model
    Difficulty: 2   Section: 1   Objective: 3

62. How does the current model of the atom differ from Bohr's model?
    Answer:
    Bohr believed electrons traveled in definite paths. The current model says that the exact path of an electron cannot be predicted.
    Difficulty: 2   Section: 1   Objective: 2

63. What happens if the number of electrons and protons are not equal?
    Answer:
    It becomes a charged particle called an ion.
    Difficulty: 1   Section: 2   Objective: 6

64. What is the effect of electromagnetic force?
    Answer:
    Objects that have the same charge repel each other and objects with the opposite charge attract each other. The electromagnetic force holds the electrons around the nucleus.
    Difficulty: 2   Section: 2   Objective: 6

65. What would happen to a nucleus containing two or more protons if the strong force was absent?
    Answer:
    The nucleus would fly apart.
    Difficulty: 2   Section: 2   Objective: 6

66. Calculate the number of neutrons in carbon-12.
    Answer: 6   Difficulty: 2   Section: 2   Objective: 4

67. If the diameter of an atom is 100,000 miles, what is the diameter of its nucleus?
    Answer: 1 mile   Difficulty: 2   Section: 2   Objective: 1

68. Is it possible to have carbon atoms with different numbers of protons? Explain.

    Answer:
    No. All atoms of an element have the same atomic number, the number of protons in the nucleus of an atom.

    Difficulty: 2   Section: 2   Objective: 3

69. What three things happen to radioactive atoms after a certain amount of time?

    Answer:
    They spontaneously fall apart. As they fall apart, they give off smaller particles as well as energy.

    Difficulty: 1   Section: 2   Objective: 4

70. What error did Thomson find in Dalton's atomic theory?

    Answer:
    Thomson discovered that atoms are made of smaller parts.

    Difficulty: 1   Section: 1   Objective: 1

71. What is the name for Thomson's model of the atom?

    Answer:
    the "plum-pudding" model

    Difficulty: 1   Section: 1   Objective: 3

72. What is the current model of the atom called?

    Answer:
    the electron-cloud model

    Difficulty: 1   Section: 1   Objective: 3

73. What is an atom's mass number equal to?

    Answer:
    the total number of protons and neutrons in that atom

    Difficulty: 1   Section: 2   Objective: 5

74. How is the atomic mass of an element calculated?

    Answer:
    by taking a weighted average of the mass numbers of the isotopes of that element

    Difficulty: 1   Section: 2   Objective: 5

75. How do isotopes differ from one another?

    Answer:
    in the number of neutrons they have

    Difficulty: 1   Section: 2   Objective: 4

MATCHING

    a. atomic number   f. mass number
    b. proton   g. weak force
    c. strong force   h. ion
    d. neutron   i. electron
    e. isotope   j. gravitational force

76. _____ particle of the nucleus with no electrical charge

    Answer: D   Difficulty: 1   Section: 2   Objective: 2

77. _____ negatively charged particle

    Answer: I   Difficulty: 1   Section: 2   Objective: 2

78. _____ keeps a nucleus with two or more protons from flying apart

    Answer: C   Difficulty: 1   Section: 2   Objective: 6

79. subatomic particle that has a positive charge
   Answer: B   Difficulty: 1   Section: 2   Objective: 2
80. ____ pulls objects toward one another
   Answer: J   Difficulty: 1   Section: 2   Objective: 6
81. ____ atom that has the same number of protons as other atoms of the same element do but that has a different number of neutrons
   Answer: E   Difficulty: 1   Section: q2   Objective: 4
82. ____ a charged atom that forms when the numbers of electrons and protons are not equal
   Answer: H   Difficulty: 1   Section: 2   Objective: 6
83. ____ represents the sum of protons in the nucleus of an atom
   Answer: A   Difficulty: 1   Section: 2   Objective: 3
84. ____ enables a neutron to change into a proton and an electron in certain unstable atoms
   Answer: G   Difficulty: 1   Section: 2   Objective: 6
85. ____ the sum of the protons and neutrons in an atom
   Answer: F   Difficulty: 1   Section: 2   Objective: 5

a. atomic number   f. neutron
b. nucleus   g. atom
c. electron cloud   h. electron
d. mass number   i. atomic mass unit (amu)
e. isotope   j. proton

86. ____ particle than cannot be cut
   Answer: G   Difficulty: 1   Section: 1   Objective: 3
87. ____ negatively charged particle discovered by Thomson
   Answer: H   Difficulty: 1   Section: 1   Objective: 1
88. ____ central region of the atom
   Answer: B   Difficulty: 1   Section: 1   Objective: 1
89. ____ region where electrons are likely to be found
   Answer: C   Difficulty: 1   Section: 1   Objective: 2
90. ____ particle in the center of an atom that has no charge
   Answer: F   Difficulty: 1   Section: 2   Objective: 2
91. ____ subatomic particle that has a positive charge
   Answer: J   Difficulty: 1   Section: 2   Objective: 2
92. ____ a unit of mass that describes the mass of an atom or molecule
   Answer: I   Difficulty: 1   Section: 2   Objective: 5
93. ____ the number of protons in the nucleus of an atom
   Answer: A   Difficulty: 1   Section: 2   Objective: 3
94. ____ atom that has the same number of protons but different numbers of neutrons
   Answer: E   Difficulty: 1   Section: 2   Objective: 4
95. ____ the sum of protons and neutrons in an atom
   Answer: D   Difficulty: 1   Section: 2   Objective: 3

a. electron   c. neutron
b. proton

96. ____ positively charged particle
   Answer: proton   Difficulty: 1   Section: 2   Objective: 2
97. ____ negatively charged particle
   Answer: electron   Difficulty: 1   Section: 2   Objective: 2
98. ____ uncharged particle
   Answer: neutron   Difficulty: 1   Section: 2   Objective: 2
a. atomic mass unit   c. mass number
b. atomic number   d. atomic mass

99.   sum of the protons and neutrons

    Answer: C   Difficulty: 1   Section: 2   Objective: 5

100. ____ mass of an atom expressed in atomic mass units

    Answer: D   Difficulty: 1   Section: 2   Objective: 5

101. ____ describes the mass of an atom

    Answer: A   Difficulty: 1   Section: 2   Objective: 5

102. ____ number of protons in the nucleus

    Answer: B   Difficulty: 1   Section: 2   Objective: 3

ESSAY

103. Long ago, people tried to change inexpensive metals, such as lead, into gold. What fundamental principle of matter did these people fail to understand?

    Answer:

    These people did not understand that elements, such as lead and gold, are divided into smaller particles called atoms. Each atom of an element is composed of a unique number of protons, neutrons, and electrons. Atoms cannot be created or destroyed. Therefore, it is not possible to simply convert one metal into another.

    Difficulty: 3   Section: 1   Objective: 1, 2

104. The ionosphere is a region of Earth's upper atmosphere. From the name ionosphere, what can you conclude about the gases that make up this region?

    Answer:

    The ionosphere must contain ions, which are electrically charged particles. To be charged, the numbers of electrons and protons in the particles must not be equal.

    Difficulty: 3   Section: 2   Objective: 3, 6

PROBLEMS

105. The approximate composition of naturally occurring magnesium is as follows: 79% magnesium-24, 10% magnesium-25, and 11% magnesium-26. Calculate the atomic mass of magnesium. Show your work.

    Answer:

    $(0.79 \times 24) + (0.10 \times 25) + (0.11 \times 26) = 24.32$ amu

    Difficulty: 2   Section: 2   Objective: 5

INTERPRETING GRAPHICS

Use the diagram below to answer the following four questions.

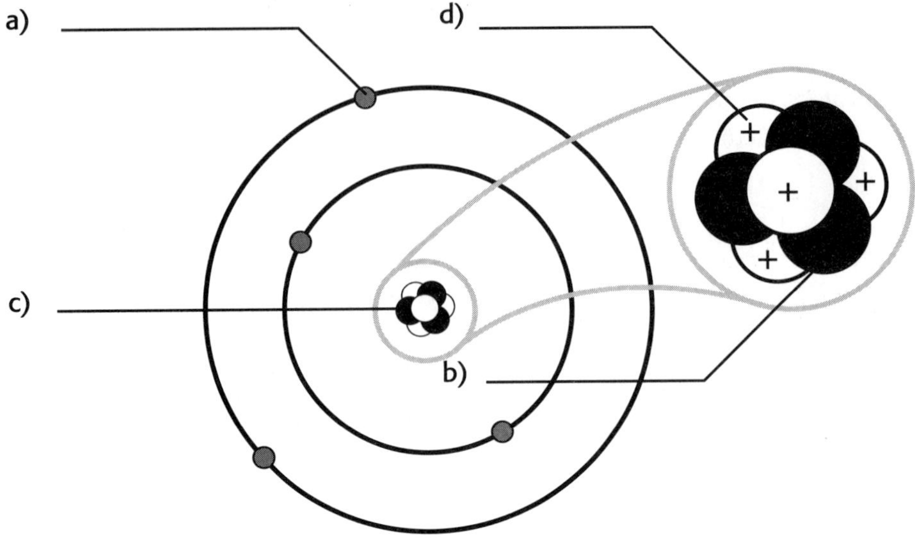

106. Which letter refers to the negatively charged particles?

    Answer: B   Difficulty: 1   Section: 2   Objective: 2

107. Which letter refers to the positively charged particles?

    Answer: A   Difficulty: 1   Section: 2   Objective: 2

108. Which letter refers to the particles with no charge?

    Answer: D   Difficulty: 1   Section: 2   Objective: 2

109. Which letter refers to the dense center of the atom?

    Answer: C   Difficulty: 1   Section: 2   Objective: 2

Use the figure below to answer the following two questions.

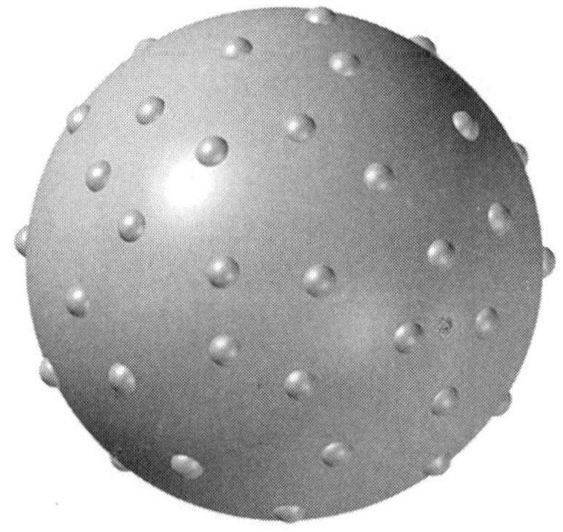

110. Who proposed this new model of an atom?

    a. Bohr   c. Rutherford

    b. Thomson   d. Democritus

    Answer: B   Difficulty: 1   Section: 1   Objective: 2

111. The raised surfaces show

    a. protons.   c. neutrons.

    b. electrons.   d. isotopes.

    Answer: B   Difficulty: 1   Section: 1   Objective: 3

9997282280 1 2 3 4 5 6